# How to Master

# This Game Called Money

**A Blueprint For Financial Freedom**

I0172432

**Authored By**
**John Jester**
Copy@2016
Rivised@2019, @2023

**BSB**
**BROWN STONE BOOKS**

**Published by**
**Brown Stone Books LLC**
**680 US Highway 130**
**PO Box 9714**
**Hamilton, NJ 08650**
**716-508-0752**

## Disclaimer

This Manual was designed to educate and provide general information for guidance regarding the subject matter covered inside. However, laws and practices often vary from state to state and are subject to change. Because each factual situation is different, specific advice should be tailored to the particular circumstance. For this reason, the reader is advised to consult with his or her own advisor regarding that individual's specific situation.

The author has taken reasonable precautions in the preparation of this book and believes the facts presented in the book are accurate as of the date it was written. However, neither the author nor the publisher assume any responsibility for any errors or omissions. The author and publisher specifically disclaim any liability resulting from the use or application of the information contained in this book, and the information is not intended to serve as legal advice related to individual situations..

## Dedication

I'd like to dedicate this book to my wife Marlene Jester and my mother Bertha Ann Jester.

To Mom, who always encouraged me with my entrepreneur projects, even when they were not having any kind of success or making money. She always encouraged me to keep going and supported me while sometimes being my only customer.

And, of course to my wife Marlene, who always pointed out my ability to be able to sit down and write letters and contracts on the spot to someone during both personal and business ventures. She recognized my ability to write this book long before I was able to realize it. It is with her uplifting encouragement that I was able to start and finish this project. She gave tremendous support even while this book was being written during some highly stressful times in our life. The completion of this book is very clear evidence for us that even under negative moments in life or as they say in the darkest of days, something very good can still come out of it. Those negative days that could've broken many couples, turned out to be like Super Glue for bonding us.

Blessings!!

Thanks Marlene and Mom! Love ya!!!!!

**How to Master this Game Called Money**

Table of Contents:

About The Author

Born and raised in Trenton, NJ John Jester has learned some of the secret/simple and untaught strategies to learn how to master this game called money. John Jester has taught some of these strategies in seminars and coaching sessions to help other people learn how to empower themselves financially and retire early. These basic strategies are the same strategies that he uses to form a simple blueprint for financial independence. John is on a mission to help 100 families a year obtain financial freedom. To obtain this goal, he must first educate people and undue the purposely misguided teachings that have been instilled in many people in the financial arena and other areas.

How To Master This Game Called Money is only the beginning. It's part one of a two-step process to obtaining Wealth. John believes that part one can be accomplished by all of the working-class people that are willing to be committed, work harder and smarter, and most importantly, have the burning desire to want to be financially FREE! Part two of this process will be focused on Building Wealth. John believes that wealth building is not for everyone, and this is why these instructions are being placed in two separate books. Building Wealth requires a different mindset, strategies and internal desire of each individual. This is not for everyone, and this is the main reason that this book focuses solely on Financial Freedom and not Wealth Building. Most people are interested in becoming financially free so they can be able to spend their time doing what they love to do. This is something that they can accomplish with part one (How To Master This Game Called Money).

## Chapter 1

### Money has no Alliance

Do you know why you should master this game called money?
Do not worry, most people don't. I believe that it is common that
most people have never considered the thought of mastering money.
It appears as though most people focus on working to obtain it and
then use it to pay their bills and/or luxuries that they may desire.
The mere thought of mastering money never occurs to the average
person.

Here is something to think about. (Food for thought) Simply put,
Money is Neutral. It has no desired destination. It only functions on
the will and desire of others, so if you do not master the money, it
will become your master.

What do I mean by that? The Master in the early days of America,
roughly early 1500's until arguably the 1900's, the newly titled
"Americans" used Africans as their tools to mine their personal
Property & Businesses. These Africans were considered Slaves in
the eyes of their keepers which they called their "Masters". The
African Slaves or POW's sole purpose each day was to be the
servant of their masters and complete tasks given to them by their
Master. On the other hand, the Masters of these slaves had
inherently set themselves up as becoming the tools of Money:
Therefore, becoming Slaves to the Money. You see in their quest for
the MONEY they had given up their integrity in exchange for Power
and control, which resulted in MONEY. Although some had
profited a great deal, there were still a large number of
settlers/immigrants or as they are called now (Americans) that did
not profit as well, but yet they were still masters to the African
prisoners of war that they called slaves.

You see, in their quest for riches and the idea of money, they had
emotionally become slaves to the money.

I believe that money is neutral, it does not really have any power. We give it power. I believe that it is okay to obtain as much money as you want, for it is not the money that is good or bad, it is the person, how they use it and/or how they obtained possession of it that gives the ideal of good or bad. So, if you are pursuing money, don't look at the money as your final goal, try to see the purpose, the reason for why you want to obtain the money. It should not be a goal to just say, "I want a lot of money", it's really the journey along the way and what it makes of you. Yes, it's the person that you become along the way to obtain the money. Are you happy with that person? Are you happy with the way you obtained the money? Did you obtain your money in an honorable way? Did you have to step on anyone in pursuit of getting it? Did you enslave anyone in pursuit of getting your money? What type of person have you or will you become with the pursuit of this money? What impact did you make, or can you now make to others? What sacrifices did you have to make? These are some real questions that you may encounter during your life Journey.

In this book, I'm going to talk to you about the use of Money here in America and it's affect throughout the world. I'm also going to give you some reasons why you should master this game called money and why you SHOULD BE FINANCIALLY FREE.

Now understand, while reading this book, it is very important to read through each chapter in its exact order. It is important that you do not skip through because each section is specifically meant to take you up the mountain one step at a time, and as you know, if you try to skip steps in life, you can get tripped up and hurt yourself. Seriously, these steps are meant to build a foundation for you as you move towards your newly discovered riches. Believe it or not, Riches are already embedded within you. Before the end of this book, hopefully, you'll come to realize it.

When starting from the beginning, I have to use my life, my experiences, and my encounters of other people's experiences to get you started.

I remember growing up in Trenton, NJ in a semi attached 2-bedroom house. A semi attached would be comparable to what some places call a Duplex. It's a building with 2 separate family entrances. (one on the left & one on the right) Both of our sides had a main floor, 2nd floor where the 2 bedrooms and bath were and we also had a basement below the first floor. In addition to the house, we had a pretty good size backyard for running around and playing. Living at the 2 bedroom house was me of course, my Mother, Sister, my Aunt, her son, (cousin) and our matriarch, my Grandmother Ann Robinson.

A little history of this house:
This house was given to my grandmother by her mother (my great grand) who had received it from the people she had worked for. Yes, she worked for a family for many years and served that family until the family moved out of the house into a bigger and better neighborhood. I don't know all of the small details, but it is said that my great grandmother was given the house as a gift or a very nominal amount just for being a good servant to this family for many years. This house was passed from my great grandmother to my grandmother. My grandmother then passed it on to my mother and mom finally passed it on to me. A lot of history in this house.

Going back one more generation, my great grandmother's mother, who I believe would be my great great grandmother, right? Her name was Indian Ann of Indian Mills, New Jersey. It is said that she had 100 acres or more of land here in NJ in Burlington County. This land was taken or lost to the Government, so as a result, her children, which included my great grandmother, her siblings and all of their heirs never had the opportunity to benefit from any of great great grandmother Indian Ann's heritage land. I mention this because it plays a part into what we'll be talking about in the upcoming chapters and hopefully you should understand even more of why you should Master This Game Called Money.

Now back to the 2-bedroom house.

As I was growing up in the 2-bedroom house, I was too young to understand the importance of learning how to Master The Money Game, but looking back, I can see how many of the events framed my mind and my attitude towards money. You may be wondering how so many people were living in a 2-bedroom house. I wonder that myself sometimes looking back, but we made it through. My mother and aunt occupied the back bedroom while my cousin, sister and I slept in the front bedroom with grandmother. I remember grandma having a huge bed and the three of us (kids) would sleep with her in her bed every night.

My mother & my aunt appeared to be back and forth in and out of the house living the single life while my Grandmother held down the household with my cousin, my sister and myself. They would both leave the house for a while and eventually come back to live in grandma's house. All the time, we would still be taken care of by grandmom and still sleep in the king size bed with her.

My Aunt eventually moved out and purchased a house in North Trenton on Wayne Ave. She took my cousin with her, and this left us with 4 remaining at the house. I don't remember all of the details of why, but the next person to leave the house was my mother. She moved out and my sister and I was left there with our grandmother. Now, still young and with my aunt, cousin and mother no longer living at the house, my sister and I were able to move into the back bedroom. We finally had our space. We were able to each have our own twin size bed. This was a big deal. Life went on. Grandma continued to raise us while my mother made frequent visits back to the house and we would make visits to my aunt's new house. Years later, my aunt moved out of the Wayne Avenue house and purchased another house in West Trenton on Moreland Ave. She did not sell the Wayne Ave house; she kept it and rented it out for additional income.

Not knowing this at the time, but this was my first exposure to being an entrepreneur and building passive income. We'll talk more about this topic further in the book. Just know that for now, I'll be making reference to two types of income.

1. Earned Income, which the majority of people have. This is where you exchange time for money. Yes, you give up hours of your life for a particular amount of money. Either lump sum or more commonly people are paid by the hour.

2. The second type of Income that you will hear me speak on is Passive Income. This is where money can be paid to you on a weekly, monthly or quarterly basis without you having to exchange your time for the money. This money can come into your bank account month by month without you having to work that month. Similar to dividends from a stock, royalties from a Movie or Record deal, or rent from a Rental Property that you control.

Back to the house:

Of course, everything was not peaches and cream, living in a crowded house and being a duplex, I remember the crazy bug problems that we use to have. Still today, I can see them as clear as if it was yesterday. When entering the Kitchen at night, hitting the switch and watching the roaches just run in all different directions. Pretty funny now, but It was scary when I first saw them. I eventually adjusted and got used to them and began to play games with the lights by turning them on to make them run and then cutting the switch off and being very quiet to make them think that the coast was clear and then "Boooo" turn the switch back on again. It was funny watching them scattered all over the place.

I also remember the Life Insurance man coming around to collect the money. He would go door to door in the neighborhood collecting small payments from everyone to keep their life insurance in place. There were times when grandma did not have the money or did not want to pay at that time, and she would say "don't answer that door". We would hide very quietly in the house as the Insurance man knocked and knocked on the door. I can also remember the numbers man coming around to collect money. My grandma would have her dream book and she spent lots of money every day trying to win the "Big one" as she would say. I never really knew just how much money she had, she just appeared to have money coming and going.

# How To Master This Game Called Money

As a youngster, I thought my grandmother was rich because she had worked at General Motors and always appeared to have some cash on hand. Some money would be in a coat in the closet, under the bed mattress, hidden in the bedroom closet, hidden in a jar in a cabinet. Many hiding places throughout the house. I remember my chores were to take out the garbage and keep up with the yard work. One day I asked my grandmother about getting a swimming pool for our backyard. Surprisingly, she came through. She not only purchased a swimming pool, she purchased an in-ground pool. She also let me get involved in the process of choosing the pool. I remember we were in the office preparing the documents to be signed for the purchase and grandma had worked out all of the details with the owner of the company. i.e., payment and when they were going to start digging. I remember the salesperson asking my grandma, was there anything else we can get for you? My grandma said to him, yes, I've been admiring that picture of the Golden Lion on the wall behind you. Where did you get that? The salesperson explained to her about the picture and where he obtained it and stated that the store no longer existed. My grandma said to him, wow that would surely look great in my living room. The salesperson laughed as my grandma was nodding her head and repeating herself. The salesperson said, ok we're just about done, is there anything else we can do for you? She said yes, I sure would like to have that picture in my living room. The salesperson laughed as he again explained that the store, he purchased the Golden Lion from no longer existed.

My grandma then said to him, "You asked me if there was anything else you could do before we completed the paperwork, right?" The salesperson said "yes", Grandma said "well you could add that picture to the deal." The salesperson "said, but ma'am, it's not for sale." Grandma said "yes" I understand, but you asked me if there was anything else and I gave you an answer." She asked him if that was something for the office or was it a family gift? He said, "it was for his office." She said "fine, now we can wrap this up and get started with building my pool." Needless to say, we completed the paperwork, and the salesman gave the picture to my grandma.

We had our in-ground swimming pool put in and as far as I can remember we were the only ones in the neighborhood with an in-ground swimming pool.

As you can probably guess this led to a great number of backyard cookouts for us and our neighbors, not to mention the new friends that were added because of the new swimming pool. Those were some great years and soon things were about to change. My grand mom became ill and eventually passed on.

My mother (Bertha Ann Jester) stepped up like a champ. She came back to the house and took control of raising us. Mom became the new matriarch and guide for living life. We were super blessed to have her! If not for Mom, who knows which way our lives could've gone after grandmom passed. Mom really did a great job in raising us, keeping us grounded and being a positive influence/role model for my sister and I. Love them both. I wish they both could be here to see the results of the love and great job that they did for all of us.

So, as we are getting started on our journey of why you should master this game called money, you may be wondering, that's an interesting story (maybe or maybe not) but what does this have to do with money?

The answer may be surprising to you but yet it's pretty simple. It appears much of what we learn about money and the treatment of it, comes from our upbringing. More specifically what we witness, and what we are taught. As a matter of fact, most of what we witness is what we are taught. Most people would probably think that we learn about money while being at school. Well, school is just a small portion of it as we really may get 45 mins a day for a semester during an economics class.

When you think about it, that's not really much compared to all of the everyday advertising that you are influenced by in your daily life with television, radio, newspapers, magazine ads, your family, your friends and their families. The real lessons come from those situations.

So, what do we learn? That is the big question. Both at Home and in School.

The reason why I started off telling you about my past as a youngster growing up in Trenton, NJ is because my past played a major part influencing my opinion on money and the way I thought money should be treated until I had a major event happen in my life and had my "ah ha" moment as Oprah would say. Now of course I had many more events happen while growing up, but I specifically chose those examples to make a point and how they can relate to money.

As we go further along in this book, I'm going to share with you how they relate to money and also what you can do for yourself to help you master this game called money. When I spoke earlier about making sure that you do not skip any portions of this book, it's because the comparisons from one particular incident early on can be related to my suggestions that I will have for you as we go along. Earlier in life I would have looked at some of these incidents as problems, but now, because of my own personal growth, I can see them as the solutions to the problems. Now, I can look at my earlier years as preparation for my place in life today. Without all of my prior experiences, I would not be able to appreciate the lessons learned and would not have been able to see that "ah ha" moment when it came. Yes, it hit me late in life I know. Some people get it a lot quicker than I did. Some people get it later and unfortunately some people never get it at all. So In writing this book, I would like to be part of the vessel that opens that door for you to have your moment when you decide to master this game called money.

Part of mastering the money game has a lot to do with tracking/recording and passing on information from one family member to another. Passing information from one generation to another. This is a concept that used to be practiced years ago but seemed to have been lost over many generations. At least in my family and most likely in my hometown of Trenton, NJ. And many other urban communities. I can probably guess that some people might take offense to that statement and/or argue that it's not true, but it's clearly evident in the results.

It seems that with the recent generations, some information has been passed on but very little in the fashion of mastering the money game. Even today as I look around at my old community and many others, it seems as though the information being delivered is mainly focused on social acceptance, Politics, Religion and Education, or as I like to say the miseducation of education. These areas of focus in many communities are being used as shiny objects of distraction and a means of control of direction of the people.

Ok let's talk about what I shared so far. I shared with you about my great great grandmother Indian Mills Ann of which she had over 100 acres of land here in New Jersey. Every time I think about that, I think OMG how great that would be today if that had been passed down through the generations. I wonder how much it would be worth today. I also wonder what was built on this land and what we could be doing with it today? Many questions run through my mind on what happened and what could've been done. Hmmmm! Thoughts! Now, that's a situation for a power much higher than me.

I mention this situation as an example of how tracking/recording and passing information down from one family member to another comes to play and having someone with enough knowledge to know what to do. Apparently, no one in our family had the financial knowledge of what to do with the land at that time or great great grandma Indian Ann just got shafted. Who knows?

Next, let's talk about the 2-bedroom house that I grew up in. If you can recall, there were three working adults and three children living in this 2-bedroom house. Two of the adults, my mother and aunt, had left the house early in their adult life upon reaching 18-20 years of age and eventually came back for support and moved in with grandmom. They left and came back on different occasions. Meaning they moved out on their own, while we stayed with grandmother and then they would return to live back in the two bedroom house with us all.

Looking back, I can see how we are so programmed to get out of the house because it's been an indirect input into our brains during our teenage years and emphasized more as we reach adulthood of 18. Not only are we conditioned as children by society, but many of our parents have been conditioned to promote it. "When you get 18, you're either going to college, military or getting a JOB". Then, the cycle continues generation after generation.

I can remember hearing it a lot growing up and I still hear it today as parents are quick to say to their children, you'll be 18 soon, you're either going away to college, military or you have to get a job. Then the next thing is "you'll have to get your own place to live".

Ok, so what's wrong with that, you may say? That's not bad advice.

Yes, I would agree with you if you're just looking at the words, the statement itself. The problem comes with the intentions of why they should go away to college, Military or why they should get a job.

OK, Now what?

Yes, they go to college, military, now what? They get a job, now what?
Where is the plan from there? This is where the problem lies. Many parents are conditioned to believe that if they just send their children to college, everything will be ok. They'll get themselves a college degree, and then a job and everything will be "perfect".

What do you think?
So, most people 30 and over know that this model does not work for the majority of people.
As a matter of fact:
1. Most people don't even finish college.
2. Many don't finish in 4 years as they are scheduled.
3. of those that do graduate, they either have a hard time getting a job or end up getting a job in a different field of the degree that they spent 4 years and thousands of dollars to obtain.
4. If completed, now we have a degree with thousands of dollars of debt attached to it and nothing to show.

Yes, that's a big problem.

On top of that, as people are lucky enough to eventually start working a Job, maybe going from one job to another or in some rare cases land a job where they stay there until they retire. (Which is more and more rare these days I might add)

Either way, at the end of working for 30-40 plus years and living paycheck to paycheck, the great plan is to retire in the Golden Years and live off half of the income that you were already struggling with. (The 50% Pension Plan)

SO, THAT'S THE BIG PLAN, HUH?

With this plan, living the good life of the Golden Years can have you working part time at the "Golden Arches".

Just from observation, it's clear that even after working 30-40 plus years in the work field, many people are still not able to retire and live off half of their paycheck. Many people remain at work to remain financially secure, at least in their mind. The secondary plan is to retire and get a part time job to supplement their income. If all else fails, the new plan is to wait until they are eligible for social security and use that check to supplement their retirement income. This is the great "new wave" plan for retirees today. "The Social Security Balancer!" This option may be ending soon as the Social Security Benefits may not be around in the future.

Ok, What next? Now that you are retired, what is the plan? Are you going to travel the world? Go on shopping sprees at local Flea Markets? Spend more time with Family? Sit home and do nothing? Donate your money to the casino? What will be your plan?

It's unfortunate, but true, that many people will end up getting a secondary job, staying at work, or just staying home and doing nothing because their retirement income is only just enough for them to get by on a monthly basis.
Consequently, many of these people are no longer working and they are still surviving paycheck to paycheck. The only difference is instead of an earned income weekly or biweekly check from a job, it's a monthly pension and/or social security check. Hmmm, seems like the same situation that they were in while they were working.

No one mentioned that it would be like this when they were 25 years old. They left that part out of the great retirement plan.

Of course, I can go on and on about the way this system is set up and how it programs people unknowingly to become dependent on "The System". I hope by reading this book even at this beginning stage, you will be able to see the importance of how we've been programmed to go on a certain dependent path in life and more importantly, I hope that you will be able to see the importance of why you should Master This Game Called Money.

## Chapter 2

### Step One: Earn some money

Ok, now for step one, as you are learning how to master this Game Called Money, you should first make sure that you find a way to earn money. Meaning, find a way to bring income into your pocket. You can do this by way of a JOB (which you may already have) or by starting a business. At this stage, one or both will be sufficient for the moment. As you read further into this book you will learn my ultimate end strategy that I would like for you to have.

As I am writing this, I want to acknowledge to you, the reader, that I do realize that in some areas of this Country and the World, that it is harder to find employment or start a business than other areas. I also want to mention that it is harder for certain groups of people to start a business than others. I do realize this, but nonetheless, you can't let that be an excuse for you not to SUCCEED. Take a moment to think about it and find a way. There is an old saying that "If you want something bad enough, you'll find a way to get it". That statement is so true. You really have to want it bad enough.

So, we're going to continue with the notion that you have secured a way to bring income into your pocket. Now, if you are living at home with your parents, siblings, family member or friend, I strongly suggest that you stay and continue to live in that particular arrangement whether you are living for free or splitting the cost. You see, one of the things we have been conditioned to do, is packing up and leaving our Home Base as soon as we hit 18 years of age or as soon as we finish college and in my opinion that is a big mistake. This is how we are conditioned, and this is how they want us to go into the world. They call it "Getting on our own feet". In reality, "Getting on our own feet" is only the beginning of a long life struggling financial journey for most people. Yes, there are some that leave the Home Base and do pretty well, but the majority of people tend to go on struggling and are just barely making it from month to month. We know this better described as living "paycheck to paycheck".

The "Sell" on this whole lottery mentality method is by taking the few of the people that make it and use them to promote/show the rest of the population that it is possible so that they will continue with promoting this false ideology that this is the best way to go, when in reality it is the exact method that financially entraps you. So, if you have it within you, if it is at all possible, try to stay Home and work on some of these fundamental practices that we are going to go through within this book. Don't let other people place guilt on your conscience about you living at home or living with a roommate. If you're doing it with a specific plan in mind, it's ok. If you're at home to be a slouch, then that's not good. Get a job, get a plan or get out!

Step 1 is all about getting your foundation set up with the 60/40 rule. Keep this in mind as we will go over more details of the 60/40 rule in a little while. For those of you that are not able to stay at home due to circumstances beyond your control, a first suggestion would be to find another family member or a friend that will partner with you on this financial venture. Maybe even a roommate whereas you would be able to split the cost-of-living expenses. I realize that this may sound weird for those of you that are 30 and over and probably already out on your own, but nonetheless, I want you to unfold your arms mentally, sit back and take in this information as this could be the new beginning of the rest of your financial life.

## Chapter 3

### Step Two:  Setting your foundation

This being number two will greatly depend on whether you stay at home or have to venture out and secure another place to live as your Home Base.  Ie (Apartment, Room or House with someone else.) If you are at Home and you stay at home, then this will be step 2.  If you had to make adjustments to get another place to live then you will base your new living space (Apartment, Room or House with someone) off of the numbers in the 60/40 rule.   If the new living space fits within the parameters, then you do it.  If not, then you don't and you can make adjustments until you are able to get on the 60/40 plan.  If you find yourself in a situation where you have to live alone because finding a family member or friend is not an option, you'll have to keep it simple and not let your emotions get too involved. Do not think about how pretty the new place may or may not be, how good the neighborhood may or may not be.  Try to find a place that will fit into the parameter of our 60/40 plan.  Now of course you do not want to put yourself in a dangerous living situation, please use some discretion, but find a place suitable and within the plan.  I know from experience that It will be easy to make up an excuse that would allow you to justify spending more than the 60/40 rule, but try to stay within the blueprint. This is very important.  If you ignore the rules once, then you may be more inclined to do it again and then again and then again.  Before you know it, you'll end up in the same position as the majority of the population, living paycheck to paycheck and only a few paychecks away from being broke, homeless or going into foreclosure.  So, step 2 is all about making sure that your foundation is set up and you stay within the confines of the 60/40 plan.  Sorry, yes, you'll have to write out a budget plan.  "Awwwww man".  I know some of you don't like doing that type of stuff, but it's important to know your budget.  You need to see on paper or the computer how much you have coming in and how much you have going out.  You must be honest with yourself on where you are so you can properly schedule your financial success.

**Remember financial freedom is not by chance, "It's Planned!"**

Of course, you'll have a small few that luck up and win the lottery, get an inheritance or be a beneficiary of a life insurance policy. You'll even have a small percentage of people that receive a lot of money from being in Sports, TV, Entertainment or the Movie Industry. But this is a very small portion of society that basically luck up and come into money this way. It's funny how many people idolize this small group and try to imitate them and strive to get some of the material things that this small group of people have. Many people overspend and over leverage themselves just to be able to appear to be in that small group of entertainers/stars.

Notice I did say "appear to be". This is because for many people, it's an illusion of making it big and feeling like they are part of the financial upper class of society. In reality, many of them have only entrapped themselves on a path of financial destruction. Enjoy it while it lasts, because it will end with you being broke and/or in bankruptcy. The funny thing is, it's not only the "wannabes", meaning the average working class attempting to be in the financial upper class, this is also true for some of the financially upper class people as well. Think about it and listen as you hear time and time again of rich people going broke. Million Dollar Lottery winners going broke within 5 years or so. Movie stars, Entertainers with millions, losing it all and becoming homeless, broke, struggling on the streets, some just barely making it and some with millions still living paycheck to paycheck or royalty to royalty check. Same difference!

Why do these things happen?  It's simple.  Many of these people did not have a plan.  They did not take the time to write out what was coming in versus what was going out.  They also did not take into consideration the possibility of the cash flow from the royalties could one day stop.  Too busy living life and not thinking about planning for the future.  Basically, they did not set up a blueprint like the 60/40 plan and did not Master this game called money.  They pretty much just rode along until they could not ride any longer and financially fell off of the horse.

### Chapter 4
### Step Three:
### If I knew back then, what I know now!

Start a part time business as soon as you can. What I mean by starting a part time business is, starting something that will allow you to make money while you still maintain your full time JOB. For example, I remember when I started working full time for the State of New Jersey many years ago. While in the computer room, a friend approached me about making some extra money on the side. Nothing to do with working at my State JOB. He invited me to a meeting that they were having and said that this meeting would explain more details of making money. I agreed and attended. What I observed was my first experience at MLM (Multi Level Marketing) also known today as Network Marketing. It totally blew me away. I truly did not understand it at the time, but it sure did look good and people in this business were making a lot of money. More money than I was making at that time. Now remember, I'm still living at home at this time and I did not have a clue of what the 60/40 rule was. I never heard of it. Mainly because it wasn't formally around at that time. You are hearing this for the first time as it was created while getting myself set up for financial freedom. There are other similar blueprints out there, but I did not have one at that time. I took what I learned in life and applied it to what you are now learning as the 60/40 plan.

Back in the day, I did not know anything about any rules or plans. I only knew of "work", "make money" and "spend it". That was the full extent of my knowledge. Sad but True! Unfortunately, this may be the same for many other people in our society as well with one added bonus. Many people live by "Work, Make Money, and Pay My Bills".

What happened with that MLM? Well, because of my lack of knowledge, I made a decision to quit my job with the State and pursue this business opportunity. Since I was living at home, I did not have the normal pressures of having Bills due each month. I only had the unnecessary expenses that I had created in order to look good, be cool and have fun. i.e. Car, The best Car Speaker System, Clothes, Credit Cards and other useless gadgets. The business was exciting and good at first but did not bring in a weekly paycheck like I was used to, so again because of my lack of knowledge, I made another bad decision, I decided to quit the MLM business and pick up a part time job that was paying me weekly in order to meet my "little expenses & fake baller spending habit". This weekly money was Guaranteed! "Oh boy", the pressure of society was on. If I had known better, I would've stayed in the business, stayed at my State JOB, educated myself on money and worked on building that business on a part time basis until I was properly financially positioned to leave my State JOB. Duh, silly me. More on that type of business strategy in another chapter.

It's been close to 30 years and that company is still around. Today I think about it and wonder if I had stayed in the business and knowing what I know now about educating and empowering yourself, I could've easily been making a half of a million dollars per year or more today working from home, retired or semi-retired right from home. It's unbelievable how the lack of knowledge can hurt you. They say what you don't know, won't hurt you. I can surely make a pretty good argument about that not being totally correct. At the same time, I also know that we all go through a variety of experiences for a reason and with lessons learned along the way. The key point to that last sentence is the "lessons learned". I think it is vital that we pick up on the lessons and learn from them. Many times, we tend to focus on other things that are not of importance and miss the lessons that were meant for us to learn and grow.

Yes, sometimes "we the people" get caught up in the distractions of the bad events that happen in our lives and miss the lessons that are there to help us get to the next part of our journey. I see this a lot with friends, family and coworkers where people stay so focused on the negative part of the event, they never realize the opportunity or lesson that can be taken from that event in their life. Therefore, they stay in the mist of the tornado and continue to repeat certain things over and over again and never grow financially, personally, emotionally, or spiritually.

Now back to my work story:

Here I am now working part time without the MLM Business and a lot of free time. This led me to work full time again and then I eventually picked up a second JOB to make more money. Totally crazy right? What a continued spinning world I was creating for myself. As I am writing this book, I can recall this destructive financial pattern that I was creating for my life. During those years, I can recall working in various Jobs like 7-11, Wawa, several Gas Stations as an attendant, and even at a Steel Factory working various types of job duties.

I was not afraid to work. I always had some sort of a job whether full time or part time. I just did not understand or really know where I was going. I guess you can say I was just living for that moment. Jobs would come and jobs would go. The money would come in on payday and would be spent before the next payday. Does any of this sound familiar? The bad thing about this as I look back is I was still living at home with Mom. I did not have the normal adult bills like gas, electricity, mortgage, rent, water, child care, etc.... Those things were not even a part of my expenses. Man, I had it good back in those days and didn't realize it!

Now here I go again, working my multiple jobs in different locations and not really getting anywhere. I can only imagine that I must have had a desire to want more out of life. Especially after being exposed to that business opportunity some years ago.

One night while up in the wee hours of the morning, I was watching an "Infomercial". For those of you that do not know, an Infomercial is a paid advertisement that comes on Television normally in the late night/early morning hours which demonstrates a particular product or services like a Juicer, Makeup, Hair Products, Home fixit/Remedy Products, Real Estate and a whole lot more... We've all seen them; some just don't know the term that they are called.

Which one got to me? It was the Real Estate bug. I was watching this real estate infomercial and the guy on this program was speaking about the economy and teaching people how good it was to invest in real estate to generate a lot of money and to build wealth. He even went as far as showing "real people" (So I thought) and they gave testimonials which made this program sound even better. I can remember being on the couch in a very relaxed position and then making the shift to sitting up on the edge of the couch and thinking, "I can do this". These men and women are on this television show talking about how they were broke, in serious debt, homeless and other stories where they came from the bottom and made money in real estate just by using this guy's program. So, I thought, I'm going to call the number. Yes, I did it! I called the number; gave them my checking information and it was on. I impatiently waited for my program to arrive in the mail. When it came, I was super excited and immediately dove in headfirst reading and listening to the cassette tapes. Yes, I did say cassette tapes. lol   I know some of you reading this may not even know what a cassette tape is. but it was the next best thing after the "LP Records" and "8 Track Tapes" which by the way, I still have some of them. This is just before the CD/DVD era.

So I dive in head first into this program, taking notes, reading and listening to all of the information that needs to be done to get rich with real estate and I completed the course. Then, after completing the course, I can remember thinking that this is a lot of work that has to be done. It's not as easy as I thought it was going to be.

I remember putting the course down along with my notes saying that I needed some time to think about if I wanted to do this because of the time and work that would be required to do this. I thought that I was going to get rich quick! So, I pretty much sat the course down and it collected dust in a cabinet somewhere. I didn't even attempt any of the steps in the course as instructed. So, I continued working my jobs, paying whatever little bills I had and living the life, so I thought.

While I was working, I still had this desire to get rich, be wealthy or live the lifestyle of the rich and famous that I would see while watching television. (It was a very popular TV show at the time.) I was a hard worker, and I was taught that if you work hard, you could become rich just like the people on television. Since I only knew what I knew, I continued to work hard at my full time and part time jobs.

Now a year in a half to 2 years pass and I'm up late at night again and guess what's on the television in the wee hours of the morning? Yes, it's that same real estate guy with his infomercial and now he has the new and improved version. This new version is now upgraded from Cassette Tapes to CD's, DVD's and it's better than ever. I thought "Marlene, we're going to be Rich". So after I finished watching the program and seeing the new colorful graphics and a different set of people with more testimonials, I decided to buy the program again. Yes, I did it again. Bang! They got me twice. So what did I discover, you may ask? Well, after going through the course again, I would say even midway through the course, I began to realize that a good portion of the information was the same from the cassette tape version.

I mean I actually dusted off my first course and compared the two. The majority of both courses were the same, except for a couple of additions, newer forms, and different testimonials from people. At first, I thought, how could I've been tricked into buying this course again? Then, I thought wow, this guy is still selling these courses even after a couple of years, and he's still on TV. "Somebody is making money somewhere" This course has not changed and although the testimonials were different people, the stories were still the same. (From struggle to wealth) That's what I wanted I said. So since this information was still the same and nothing had changed, I thought that maybe I was the problem. I thought that maybe I had to be the one that had to change. I had to change the way I looked at this situation, "this situation?" really "my situation" and what it was going to take for me to change it. So I made a mental shift, changed my mind, kept both programs and started with the assignments in the back of the course to implement real estate investing and get me started on a personal development journey.

It had to be close to two years dipping and dabbing into the lessons before my wife Marlene and I purchased our first house.

While our real estate journey has been a great journey filled with many lessons, I'm not going to go into all of the details at this time because this book is not about real estate, it's about you having your breakthrough and mastering the money game.

I don't want you running off and investing in real estate just yet. That can possibly be in a future book. As a matter of fact, it will be in a follow up wealth strategy to this book. For now, I'll give you some information towards the end on our reference page for those of you that are ready now and have implemented what you learned with the 60/40 plan. Then you can take the next leap into the big game. "One step at a time Grasshopper"

So why do I share all of this with you for step three? It's because, depending on where you are today in your life with your struggle, with your comfort zone, and/or with your personal development, you may need a "Breakthrough". This will vary for everyone but will be similar to many. The "breakthrough" or as some say, is that "ah ha moment", is the key to change. It is the key to taking you from one level in your life to the next and it's the key to your growth. If you are not able to get pass this moment, then nothing that I teach you about winning this game called money will matter. You will only sabotage yourself. This is why I am writing this book in this specific order so I can prepare you for the winning formula. In order for you to see it, your eyes have to be open. You have to be able to see outside of the matrix that many people are in and see things for what they really are and not the perception.

**Chapter #5**

## Reflections

At this point in the book, I think that it's important for you to reflect back on what you've read so far and for you to think about how, if any of this relates to events in your life. Also, you should now begin to think about where you are. Are you living at home? On your own? Married? Renting? Mortgage? What is your status as to step one and step two?

Where are you with step three? Do you work one job? Do you work two? Do you have a part time or full time Business? Have you ever read or listened to any personal development training? Have you ever had that "Breakthrough or ah ha moment"?

Write these things out along with your goals that you want to achieve for yourself, your family, neighborhood, the world, etc...... During the next section, we're going to help you with your goals. (Step 4)

For now, stop reading and take the time to write out where you are using the questions above. It's important not to just read the information in this book, I want you to actually implement it. (Take action) As for you left brain thinkers that need to know everything before you try something, continue reading and you'll have to come back when you finish the entire book. Just know that it's always a good idea to take notes and write an outline as you go along so you do not miss any parts.

Now if you are still reading this without stopping and writing down your goals, you may have just identified yourself as a left-brain thinker. I totally understand. Don't worry, Right Brain or Left Brain, no one can really say which one is better, it's just a way of identifying who will take action right away and who will try to get all of the information first before taking action. I don't believe that one way is better than the other. Sometimes it's good to have all of the information and sometimes it's good to take action as you go along. There are pros and cons on both sides. I did this so you can see where you are. So, if you simply continued reading without taking the time out to do the assignment, you'll probably be leaning more towards a left brain person. You know what I mean: Logical, Critical Thinking, Reasoning, need to see all of the numbers! Recognize it and then implement the best strategy that you can according to your right or left brain.

During this book, I may ask you to do certain tasks along the way. No worries, if you are one that has to read through continually and then complete the task later, do yourself a favor and at least highlight the area or mark it so when you reread this book it will make your task completion much easier.

## Chapter #6

### Step 4:  Set your Goals

Where do you want to go?  Write it out.  What do you want out of life?  It should be something.  If it is nothing and you do not want any more out of life than what you already have, STOP NOW!  You shouldn't even be reading this book because it is for those that want to achieve more, have more, find themselves, help and/or empower other people.  This is for people that want to do the things that they would love to do without the pains and stress of having to go to work every day to make a living and/or pay bills.

My belief again is, if you solve the MONEY problem, you'll be able to focus on the things that matter the most to you.  (Family, spiritual, fun, service to others)

Money is only paper, for now at least.  It's just an idea and the concept that our system runs on.  Don't get caught up in the idea of having money.  Focus on what the money will allow you to be able to do.  I call this the "Benefit of".  Yes, the benefit of having the money.  I don't believe that most people would simply like to have money just to be having money.  What good would it be to have a pile of money and no real use or benefit of having it.  Example:  What good will it be to have a pile of money with no friends, family, sense of spirituality, no fun, not servicing others, not being able to buy things/gadgets/gifts, traveling, etc.?  Without these things what good is the money?  Answer: It has no real beneficial value on its own.  Since money has no real value on its own and is only used to operate in our system, we will focus on the real true "Benefit of" what we want.  The Benefit Of The Benefit of having the money.

How to set your goals:

1. Make a decision on what it is that you want out of life. I would suggest that you go with your first instinct and write it down. I realize that everyone is not aware of what they truly want out of life. Especially when they are first asked to write out their goals. Keep in mind that your goals can and most likely will change as you grow and become more aware of your inner self, so don't worry about getting too deep right now. Also keep in mind that you can have more than one goal. For the moment, just write out what comes to mind first. You can write as little or as many as you want, but you should write something. (Pause and complete that)

Once you have your goal/s written out, I want you to line them up in the utmost importance. Meaning the ones that stand out the most. A must have. (Pause and complete)

Next, I want you to line them up with the ones that are monetary connected. Meaning, which ones will require a particular amount of money to obtain. Believe it or not, there are goals that do not require money. For this section, I want you to line up the goals that are most important to you and the amount of money you think it may require to obtain it. (Pause and complete)

Now that we have our goals, let's write out a short term and long-term target of completion of these goals for you to obtain. I.e. One year, five years, ten years. I'm laughing as I am writing this because I know I'm still going to have some of you thinking that "this is too much for you to do" or "you do not have to do all of this in order to make money".

My response to you if you are feeling that way would be to either stop reading NOW and start over from the beginning because it is possible that you have not had your "Breakthrough" yet and are still seeing through the eyes of the matrix, or if you think that you did have your breakthrough and you still have these feelings, then you are absolutely RIGHT! "It is too much for you" or "you don't have to do all of these things" because if that is your belief, then, that is as far as you will be willing to go. I was listening to a speaker one day and he made a statement that said "Whether you think you can or think you can't, you're probably right!" Think about that for a moment. It is not possible for you to go beyond the      point of your thoughts/beliefs. You're setting limitations of      what you can complete. If you think you can only get to a certain level or think you cannot do something, that's it. That's the way it will be. It's called "The power of CHOICE!". It's always yours and you're the one that will always decide. "To do or not do", I've been there. It's something that you have to deal with if you want to break free emotionally and to be financially FREE. (Pause and complete this section, start over to get your breakthrough if needed so you can mentally move forward. If not, you will most likely return back to where you were before you started reading this book.)

**Let me give you a basic example of what this can look like**

Reverse Engineering

OK, let's dig a little deeper with these goals.

Reverse engineering does not mean driving a car backwards. I am simply describing the method of reversing the outcome of your goal. So instead of starting from where you are today, which most people do, we're going to map it out by starting from where you want to be. For example: You have a goal of wanting a new car. Let's also say you want this new car twelve months from today. First decide on the type of car that you want, then figure out how much the car costs.

Do you want to pay cash or are you going to finance the cost? Let's use a car with a price point of twenty-five thousand dollars. Let's start with the cash option. You know that in twelve months, you want to buy your car at twenty-five thousand dollars, so the simple saving solution would be to save twenty-five thousand dollars, divided by twelve months. ($25,000 / 12 months = $2,083.33+) This means that for the next twelve months, you have to put away $2,083.33 a month and you will be able to walk into the car dealership and purchase your new car. (Give or take, taxes and misc fees not included) Congratulations, you've just reached your goal. Fairly simple right? Well, as long as you are able to save two thousand dollars a month that is.

Now let's look at the finance option. We're going to continue with the same car price of twenty five thousand dollars. If you choose to finance, you will not have to come up with the whole amount. Now, depending on your credit, you can put down 3%, 5%, 10%, 20%, etc.. and walk out with the same car in twelve months. So, in this example, let's go with the amount of 20%. To have a 20% down payment you will need a total of five thousand dollars. Reverse engineering from the goal, ($5,000 / 12 months = $416.66+) This means you will have to save $416.66 for the next 12 months and you'll be able to purchase your car. Congratulations, you've just reached your goal.

Do I want you to go out and buy a new car? Do I want you to finance it or pay cash? While that would be nice of course, that was not the point of this example. I wanted to give you a short demonstration of how to start at your goal and work your way back to the starting line of where you are today. This way you will be able to have some checkpoints along the way. You should know from month to month where you are. Are you on track or behind, simply by using the multiple saving months to chart your journey. You'll know that by saving $416.66 every month, you should be at $2,083.30 by the fifth month. If not, then you should make adjustments to get there so you can reach your goal on time.

This concept/formula works the same for all of your goals, whether they are monetary or not. Every goal should have a starting point, meaning where you are now and an end point, meaning where you want to be. It is up to you to add in the checkpoints to chart your journey and measure the progress that you are making with obtaining each goal. If you do not have checkpoints, you will not be able to tell if you are on track to reaching your goal and you will not know if you have succeeded or failed until the end of your designated time. By then, it's too late! This may not be so bad for a 14- or 30-day goal, but the longer the time period of the goal, the more potential damage to your "Will/Conscious" and the more time lost in your life. With time being your most valuable asset, this is one thing that you can't afford to lose because you cannot get any of it back. You can work with thoughts from the unconscious to the conscious, you can work with being unwilling and then have the "Will to do" again, you can also work with unknowing and then learning to do, but you once you let the time go by, you cannot get that back.

So, make the best of your time and use it every day to your fullest potential.

Although there is so much more that we can talk about with writing goals, preparing them, executing them and so on, I do not want to have you reading example after example and getting caught up in the examples. More importantly, I want you to write out your own set of goals, blueprints, checkpoints and apply them to the information that you've learned so far in this book and what you are going to learn in the upcoming chapters.

So, if you haven't done so already, I want you to "STOP" reading and write your goals out. Make sure that you have everything set up from step 1- step 4. Yes, I know that your living situation may be more complicated than just making a decision, but at a minimum you can write it down and make it part of your goal to be in a step 1 and/or step 2 position that will be more beneficial to your financial future. The reason that I want you to do this now is to make sure that you do not skip any of the steps and make sure you don't forget. If you are anything like me, when I read a book, I don't remember all of the details about the book, I mainly recall certain sections and almost always have to go back and re-read many books to retain more of the story or concepts.

So, I'm saying this to you because your financial future is too important for you to simply guess or take a chance on remembering. This is just a suggestion, but highly recommended. Also think, even if you re-read the book, just by having your goals and checkpoints already drafted and written out, it will be much easier to make adjustments rather than creating it for the first time. Together we will create your financial plan along the way as you go through the book, so when and if you do re-read, it will be much clearer the second time around.

**Chapter #7**

**Step 5:   Where does your money go?**

Now we're going to take the position that you have been a good student up until this point and have followed all of the steps from 1 through 4. Assuming that you have some goals and are making some money from your JOB and/or business, we're going to move you to the next phase.

I believe that making money for a lot of people is not the problem. I believe that it's a combination of personal development and not knowing what to do with the money after you've earned it. This seems to be a universal problem with many cultures and perhaps the main reason why such a large percentage of our population here in America struggles financially throughout their lives and usually end up on some sort of public assistance towards the end of their life or at retirement. So, without going too deep into that topic right now, we're going to continue with the next step.

Now that we have a JOB and/or a Business in place and you are of course working really hard and/or smart to earn money, I want to introduce you to a couple of terms that can change your life forever. Those terms are of course PERSONAL DEVELOPMENT, ROI, TIME FREEDOM & MARKETING and the 60/40 blueprint plan.

If I have not mentioned it before, I want to be very clear in stating that I am not a financial advisor, CPA, or an Attorney. I am simply giving you personal experience and knowledge that I've picked up on the many trials and tribulations, failures and successful ventures in my life. I cannot know the financial situations of every reader that will pick up this book and I do not know which of you are hard workers and which are not, who are the quitters and who will hang in there and do it until it gets done.

It is hard for me to predict that; therefore, I do not give any warranties/guarantees that this will work for everybody. I'm going to lay the blueprint out and leave it to you to decide if it will work for you or not. After all, if you don't believe it, then it will not work for you right? It is a must that you take it all in and follow along and map this journey out for your life and believe that you can accomplish the goals of your journey.

Now let's start with ROI.

ROI stands for "Return On Investment" Oh noooooo, I have to make investments? lol "I don't want to learn how to do investments", you may say. Yes, sorry to disappoint you but making an investment is something that can't be avoided. What you may not know my friend, is that the investment that I'm going to be talking about is not your typical type of investments like stocks, mutual funds, bonds, C. D's, etc... The investment vehicle that we're going to be talking about is the best, most valuable one of them all. That is <u>"YOU!"</u> Yes, <u>"YOU"</u> are the commodity, you are the investment which you will be betting your life on. So as the villain said in the Movie "Are you ready to Plaaaay?"

OK, let me give you the formula:

ROI- Return on Investment equals (Return from your Investment minus the Initial cost of your investment, divided by the cost of investment. Huh? You may say what does that mean?

The simplest way to explain the return on investment is to show it to you along with the formula that we use to calculate ROI. Ok, so let's say that you've invested $100 into buying some lottery tickets from the corner store. You buy $1, $2, $5 and you even splurge and pick up a couple of $10 and $20 tickets, but in total you only spend $100. Now, you may have a good time scratching the tickets, playing the Bingo games and so on. After all of the tickets are scratched off, you realize that you've won $150. Woo hooo!

So you've spent $100 and you received $150 back. At first glance, most people would say, hey, I won $150. Now, is that your return on investment? Not really.

Let's place the numbers in the formula.
ROI- Return on Investment equals (Return from your Investment minus the Initial cost of your Investment, divided by the cost of investment.
ROI= ($150-$100) divided by the initial cost of $100
ROI=($50) divided by $100
So in this case (150-100) divided by 100 = ROI
$$(50) \quad \text{divided by } 100 = .5 \text{ aka } 50\%$$

This means that you received your initial investment of $100 back plus an additional $50 which is half of what you invested. Get it? So you did not win $150, you won $50, which is good.

On the flip side, let's use the same number of the initial investment $100 and after scratching off all of the tickets and having fun, you only won $70. Some people would be happy with that and say heeeey, I won $70 on my scratch offs. Well, again, let's examine using the ROI Formula.

Let's place the numbers in the formula.
ROI- Return on Investment equals (Return from your Investment minus the Initial cost of your Investment, divided by the cost of investment.
ROI= ($70-$100) divided by the initial cost of $100
ROI=($-30) divided by $100
So in this case (-30) divided by 100 = ROI
$$(-30) \text{ divided by } 100 = -0.3 \text{ aka } -30\%$$

43

# How To Master This Game Called Money

In layman terms, this means that you invested $100 and lost $30. So if you continue to do this, you will eventually run out of money or simply continue working to earn new money in order to have a fresh $100 to invest in scratch offs. It's very similar to what we do as we place our money in our savings or checking accounts. When you place your money in a standard savings account, you are directly placing your money in a negative ROI position. The reason for this is because many savings accounts pay you less than 1% APR on your money that sits in the account while inflation is rising at a rate of 3% APR or more. APR meaning "Annual Percentage Rate".

So, if the economy/inflation is rising at 3% and your money is growing at less than 1%, can you see how you are losing money and how this will keep you in a forever money chasing position? At this rate, you'll never be able to be financially free. It's like you're running backwards. Don't forget, you also have checking accounts. Many checking accounts are free to open, but they do not pay any interest on the money that you save in these accounts, therefore if they don't pay any interest, then your money is in an even worse position than your savings account. They say that it does not cost you anything, but "oh boy" it sure does. It cost more than you know. But, now that you know after reading this book, the question is, what are you going to do about it? Everything cost something. Time, Money or Services. There is always some sort of exchange.

Now if this is new to you, don't get caught up in the fact that this is Math. Look at it as learning how to set up checkpoints for tracking and keeping up with your money. If you don't take care of your own money, someone else will do it for you. Do you remember the checkpoints that we used in the goal setting? If not, no worries, I'm going to break it down and put it in layman's terms for you just like I had to do for myself, so you're in good hands.

Looking back on when we were setting up our goals, I gave an example of working and saving money to reach a goal of buying a new car for $25,000. Remember that? Now, in that example, we worked to earn money, then we took a portion of the money and saved it in the bank, credit union, at home in a cookie jar or under the mattress, ha-ha. From there, we continued until we reached our goal of five thousand dollars for a down payment or twenty-five thousand dollars for the complete purchase.

This is what we call "working for the Money" or "earned income". We use this "working for the money" strategy in order to buy a new car, pay bills, buy toys and gadgets for ourselves or others and so on. This strategy is probably what most people are used to doing. It's embedded in us from our education system. Working for the money and then spending it on a variety of things. Some useful and really needed for oneself and a good portion of it not really useful or needed, maybe just "wanted". I believe that sometimes a person's "wants" gets in the way of what they really "need" and their "wants" strongly influences their financial spending decisions which guide them to their ultimate financial destination.

So, if you want to be able to master this game called money, you have to find a way to get your money to work for you in addition to you working for it. (Money) This is where the ROI comes in. When you think ROI, think about where and how you place your money once you receive it. Think about what you've done recently over the past six months when you had money, when you earned money, when you received your paycheck. Did you just spend it on things, give it away, or did you strategically place it so that you'll have a chance of it coming back to you plus some extra?

That is the difference between people that have money and people that don't. The more conscious that you become of this method of placing your money so that it comes back to you, the better off you will find yourself in the future financially. You have to really think when you are placing your money with someone or an institution. Is this money that I'm giving away or will I get a return on my money spending it this way? These are the things that you must think about after you receive your money and before you spend it.

Here is a simple example of one of the businesses that I use to get a positive ROI on my money. Now this is a simple version and it's something that many people can do.

Example:
I spend fifty dollars a month to have an online business active. Now keep in mind that this concept and formula will work whether it's fifty dollars, five hundred dollars or five thousand dollars per month. Apples to Apples with the formula, it will be the same. I'm using fifty dollars to show you just how attainable and simple it can be. Ok, now fifty dollars a month to open your business. Inside of your new business, with every sale that you make, you will get a 30% recurring commission of a $50 product. This means that you will be able to make a total of $15 per month of every sale that you make. Now let's get some sales. We'll start with the free marketing concept of word of mouth, social media, and maybe putting up a physical sign or banner. If you made one sale a month, this is what it would look like.

Month number 1 you make fifteen dollars ROI, which is fifteen dollars back from the fifty dollars that you just spent. That's a little something. It's a negative ROI, but it's an ROI.

Month number 2, you now have two sales and you make $15 x 2 = $30 for the month. You're still spending $50 per month to keep your business up and running, so while you are making $30 per month from your two sales, you're still in the hole $20, but it's better than spending the money on useless things that do not bring anything back to serve you or your family.

Month number 3, you make another sale. You now have 3 sales, and you make $15 x 3 = $45 per month recurring sales. At this point you are spending $50 per month and making back $45 per month. Your business is almost being paid for monthly by your three customers.

You make another sale in month 4 and that equals $60 per month recurring income. You are now in a positive ROI of your money. This means that for every $50 that you spend each month, you are getting your initial investment back of $50 plus an additional $10. This may not seem like much you may say, it's only $10. Unfortunately, many people will look at that and say the same thing. "It's only $10 profit, what's the big deal?" Well, the big deal is the ROI. Just with this little example of four sales, you have now laced your money in a vehicle that has allowed you to make not only $10, but a 20% ROI on your money for that month. Yes, imagine placing $50 in the bank and at the end of the month, you had $60 in your account. Yes, you can imagine if you want, but it's not going to happen. The most I've ever witnessed a bank giving a return on a checking or savings is 6-7%, and that was back in the eighties, just before the market crashed. But Wait! there's more!

Month number 5 equals $75 per month in sales, month 6 equals $90 per month, month 7 equals $105 per month, month 8 equals $120 per month, month 9 equals $135 per month, month 10 equals $150 per month, month 11 equals $165 per month, and the final month 12 equals $180 per month. By the end of month 12 you are still spending $50 per month for your business and receiving back $180 per month. This leaves you with a profit of $130 per month.

Your new monthly ROI equals 260%. Now, I'll let that sink in a little bit because I know for some people you're probably saying, "oh noooooo", "I don't like numbers", but I want you to keep this in mind while you are going through this process. Regardless of how you feel about numbers, "NUMBERS EQUALS MONEY". That's it! If you want one million dollars, then let's face it, that one million dollars looks like this "$1,000,000" (that is a real big NUMBER). lol   Learn to like NUMBERS and they will like you back. This simple example was totally dependent upon YOU making one sale per month to achieve that result.

We'll talk more on that later, I just wanted to point that out to you. When I say depending upon you, I really mean depending on you.

You can't blame the company that created the product, and you can't blame anyone else for you not being able to make a sale. You are your most valuable asset, and you have to be the one to make things happen. You are the commodity. Always keep in mind that getting to a million dollars starts off small with earning your first one dollar. This is why back in the day when you see a new business open up, they would take their first dollar and hang it up on a wall either in a frame or merely just tape it to the wall as a symbol of their beginning and the start of their journey to reach their goal, whether one hundred thousand or one million dollars.

Everyone must start somewhere, $1, $10 and then you grow from there.

## Chapter #8

### Step 6:   It's not about the money

WINNING THIS GAME CALLED  MONEY IS NOT
ABOUT MONEY

**Reasons for wanting to have big financial goals or
becoming wealthy.**

The reasons for wanting to have a pile of money or becoming
rich will probably vary with a lot of people, but a good
portion of people tend to have similar reasons for why they
want to become rich.  Let me give you some reasons why I
think YOU should pursue this goal of becoming rich.
Keep in mind that I believe that there are many forms of
riches, meaning riches of health, spiritual, mental, love,
family, physical, etc.... and these riches are far greater than
the riches of this green paper that we call money.  I truly
believe this to be true.  At the same time, I realize that this
world, this economy that we live and function in day to day,
operates on this concept called money and we need it to live
at a certain basic standard in many parts of the world.

With that said, I believe that we should master this game
called money so we would have the opportunity to live a
better lifestyle.  Meaning, we can position ourselves to be
able to eat better and healthier foods.  It's no secret that much
of our food supply that's eaten by the average person is
processed and or poisoned with different types of
manufactured ingredients that cause harm to our body over a
long period of time.  In this day and age, most people are
aware directly or have heard something from a friend about
our contaminated foods here in the US.

Eating healthier organic foods are definitely better for you, but most people can't afford the extra cost of having organic foods, therefore the average person makes a decision to buy the most amount of food that they can get for their money to feed themselves and their family. You really can't blame them, most people in our economy are just barely getting by and are living paycheck to paycheck and some of them are not even making it to the next paycheck. Some things just get cut back for the month and they usually play the "Peter and Paul" game where they take money from one area to pay another area and hope and pray that they can catch up on the next month. This process goes on month after month and for some, it continues year after year until the bottom falls out, whatever that may be for each family.

Some families reduce their cost of living, end up homeless, file bankruptcy, resort to illegal activities and some just stay in the hardship storm and live that way until they pass away. In addition to the food, we have the Water Problem. Not many people know about water being a big issue. It's really just becoming a more publicized topic, but it's not really new. This has been a problem for years with people drinking the tainted tap water and then the so-called answer to our problems was, "Bottled Water". This elevates our water problem to a new level. Bottled water is supposed to be the answer to the Tap Water. Question? Where does the bottled water come from? In the springs of the Mountains, they say. What Springs and what mountains? Where exactly are they? Did the Bottle Company go there and build a bottling company right next to this spring? or did they go to this spring and fill up tanks of water and transport it back to the bottling factory? If so, is the water still pure now? Do you still filter this water and or put ingredients in it to enhance the taste of this water that's been taken from this natural spring in the mountains?

Why do some mountain spring water taste different from others? Do the same tap water issues of the polluted environment, illegal dumping and other activities affect these mountain springs? This is just something to think about. So in addition to our regular water being poisoned with fluoride and our food being lased with MSG and other unknown ingredients, what do we do? We buy, eat and drink what we can afford. It's that simple. So, if we had enough money to buy or grow healthier foods, or maybe have our personal farm, we would definitely eat better and live a healthier lifestyle. This is a great reason to master this game called money.

**Another Reason To Master This Game called money Is Travel**

I used to be so surprised when I met someone that has not been outside of their State from which they live. As a matter of fact, I've met a lot of people that have never been outside of the city/town that they live in. I used to be so amazed and would think, how could they not have ever left this town before? Now, this would be understood as a young person up to the age of 18, but when I meet an adult over 30 and they have never been out of their City or State, I think that it's tragic that they have not had the chance to live life. It's tragic that they have not had the opportunity to experience other people, other cultures, and other environments.

It's just important for each of us to be able to have a vision and to be able to expand our horizons in life. The makeup of the brain is very powerful. We should realize that you cannot go beyond the vision of your thoughts. Small thoughts, isolated thoughts and lack of vision will keep you where you are and you will never grow into the person that you are meant to be. Some people call it finding your purpose. By mastering this game called money, you'll be able to travel abroad and go wherever your vision can take you.

Many people overlook this part of finding your purpose and growing into the person that you were meant to be, not knowing that this is probably the major key to your success. You see, once you have this, everything else can fall into place. This is the personal development of oneself. Get this right, get this first and during the pursuit of your goals, you'll find success. Success is not the MONEY! This is where many people get mixed up. People think that it's within the money, missing the true value of success being within YOU! Find "you" and you'll find the success. If you strive to obtain the money only, you'll miss the success, because it is in you that it lies.

This is why you hear about so many people with a lot of money that are UNHAPPY. They're not unhappy like the average person that's broke and struggling unhappily. They're unhappy because they've lost themselves or they have not discovered the success of happiness that is within them. They missed it on the way to their millions of dollars which now makes the money practically useless to them in an emotional/conscious way. Having the money is one thing but, finding your purpose and being happy is the real meaning of success. This book is called How To Master This Game Called Money because it is not just about money and I pray that you realize that the money system is really just a game. You should not only learn it, but you should master it and use it to assist you in finding your true purpose in life. You must invest in your most valuable asset, and that is YOU!

### Stress Free Living

Don't get this part confused when I say stress free. There is good stress and there is bad stress. I believe there will always be some sort of stress in your life as part of a balance in the universe. When I say stress free living, I'm talking about no more worries about getting the bills paid from month to month. No more having to rob Peter to pay Paul. No more having to buy or not buy things based on the price of the item. That's stress-free living. As a matter of fact with today's technology, many if not all of your monthly bills can be set up with automatic payments to go out from your checking account and you wouldn't have to concern yourself with bills that are due each month because you know that you have more than enough in your account to cover all of the bills and your extra activities that you desire. That is an awesome place to be, and this brings me to my final reason why you deserve to master this game called money.

### Contribution

Yes, contribution, paying it forward as we say in the industry. Being able to give back is what makes having the money worth it. You see, having the money and being able to take care of your wants and needs is one thing, but when you can give back to your family, your community and other communities throughout, that's a great feeling. That makes having the money worth the struggle of obtaining it. The hard times, the pain in getting to the point of stress-free living can bring smiles to your face when you turn it around and contribute to others. What's the point in having a stockpile of money if you can't share it with others? In addition to monetary contributions, you can also be able to give time and services in order to help others.

Sometimes, it's more than just money that people need. Sometimes it's good to give others a hand or teach them some of the techniques that you learned when you were at their stage in life. Whether financially, emotionally, spiritually, and so on. Now that you have the Time, Freedom and Money, you'll be able to contribute to society in a way much more powerful than if you were still barely making it and living paycheck to paycheck. Not to say that you cannot contribute when you are struggling, it's just that you can reach a lot more people when you have more money. All in all, it comes down to finding your purpose and knowing if it is meant for you to reach a lot of people or mainly making an influence on the people in your immediate area. One never really knows until they begin their journey.

The answer may be revealed as you travel through your life's journey, but you must seek in order to find.

These are only a couple of reasons why I feel you should master this game called money. You may probably relate to some of these reasons, or you may also have your own reasons why you should be rich or well off, as my grandmother used to say. Regardless of the reasons, you must first recognize that you do have a reason and then use that to fuel your way through all of the difficult times to come.

## Chapter #9

### Step 7  Personal Development

The missing link to the chain of success

To some people, this topic may seem like it's not important because on the surface it appears to have no monetary value, but to my surprise and I'm sure many others, the topic of personal development is without a doubt the missing link to the chain of success.  Now just to give you a visual of what I mean when I say the missing link, imagine a person that at first sight, they appear to be very gifted or talented at something.  It could be in school with education, it could be in sports, it could be with building something, they may be good with their hands, and so on.  You meet this person on day one.  You take note that this person is very gifted, maybe depending on the situation, you may even give them a compliment to let them know that you recognize their gift, but then days go by and then weeks, maybe even months go by as you continue to see or hear about this person, and you still appreciate their gift.  At some point, whether weeks, months or even years, you start to wonder, Wow!  This person is so talented, whatever happened to them?  or why is it that they cannot get to the next level?  Why didn't they make it?  Why are they still where they are?
The opportunities were there, the buzz was there, and without a doubt, this person certainly appeared to be talented enough.  What happened or went wrong?

I believe the answer to that is PERSONAL DEVELOPMENT.  Yes, I'm sure that a person's environment will play a part in this also, but when you dig deep down into it, it still falls back on personal development.  It's possible that the lack of personal development could've been his or her environment, meaning their "upbringing".  After all who knows what kind of household a person grows up in, you just never know.

As I talk about this, I recall hearing that as an excuse for many people. "You don't know what I went through growing up" or "you don't understand" or "you don't know what it's like to live in the hood", and there are plenty other excuses. Some are different, but most of them the same, even when they are different, because at the end of the day the result is the same of "Giving up"/"Failure". This is why personal development is so important. Not only for the gifted person, but the average person as well.

Surround yourself with like-minded people. With personal development being instilled in you and the people that you surround yourself with, you'll be able to position yourself to grow from within, therefore creating an environment for you to succeed at anything that you decide that you want to accomplish. You grow and the people around you grow.

Now, on the flip side, what I just stated was an awesome perfect scenario having yourself, parents and/or children all on the same page, learning and growing like one big happy family. In today's society, the chances have diminished of that being a reality for the majority of people due to the many different beliefs, opinions and the mis-education of education. So, where does that leave you? That leaves you with the task of taking responsibility for your own growth and success starting today. I say starting today, because you may or may not have heard about personal development prior to reading this book and therefore never considered the fact that you do have to grow in order to become successful. I know there are people that say, "I am who I am and I'm not going to change who I am", or some may say "That's just the way I am", "I've always been like that". Yes, I've heard that from people also. As a matter of fact, some of those same people may even excel in some areas of Education, Sports, Entertainment, Workforce, etc... It does happen, but that does not mean that they are necessarily successful. Sometimes when people see others obtain a so-called prominent position or making a lot of money, they mistakenly call that being successful.

In many cases after the game is over, the classroom has ended, the workday is over, the TV show has ended, the director says cut, and when all of the people are no longer around, some of these same people are miserable because they're still not happy. They may have the money, the fame, the status of society's title of being successful, but they are unhappy because they still have not found their purpose in life and are pretty much going along in life with no real intended destination. This is why finding your purpose and continued growth is so important for the individual. This is Personal Development. It's an ongoing journey and a rewarding one.

Never confuse having money with being successful. You can find plenty of people that are successful in life, but don't have millions of dollars or the society titles of success.
There are wives and husbands that are homemakers, teachers, blue collar & white-collar workers, construction workers, factory workers and so on that have sought out from the beginning to be in the positions that they currently are and have accomplished their goals. They knew from the beginning that this is what they wanted to do, they accomplished it and if they are totally happy/satisfied in reaching their goals, I consider these people successful. You have some people that work twenty-five to forty years on a particular job that they've set as their goal and if this means that they will remain there until they retire at age 65 or before and they're ok with it, then it's still good, they're successful.

You see being successful is not monetary, it's more about being satisfied with where you are and what you have accomplished. On the other hand, if someone is not totally satisfied with where they are as far as accomplishments or monetary, then they have to focus on their personal development and while I can go on and write a whole book on this topic, I'll leave you with this, If you are happy where you are, then enjoy it and live in the moment, but if you want to have more, you must become more. In other words, in order for things to change, YOU MUST CHANGE!!

This is the link that can connect the gifted/talented person to the right opportunity and can lead them to success.

## Chapter 10

### Step 8   Marketing

Here's my two cents on Marketing. I believe marketing is one of those key essential parts of your business that gets you from one point to the other. In other words the marketing is the part of your business that will help you grow. It will help you go from making that first dollar to making hundreds of dollars. I like to tell people that marketing is what makes your business grow so if you are not marketing your business, your business is probably not growing and if your business is not growing, then you're most likely on your way out of business. It's really just a matter of time. It will really depend on how much reserves you have when you open your business to carry you through your negative ROI months and your lack of growth.

Back in the day, people would say the way to market is "word of mouth". Yes, that may have worked back in the day for the neighborhood or town business, but in today's world, a new era has taken marketing to a whole new level. Far past the days of radio, magazines, television, billboards & newspapers. Yes, you can probably guess it by now, yup, it's the Internet. To even narrow it a little closer, I'll add in the words "Social Media". I do this because it's such a vital part of marketing these days. I'm still shocked when I meet an entrepreneur/business owner and they are still marketing with just the old school marketing. Just to be clear, I'm not saying that the old school methods don't work, I'm simply saying that there is a better solution today.

If you think about it, there's no difference from the early days when people "really really" only marketed using word of mouth. Passing the news around from person to person until the masses of the townspeople knew of the news. Then, one day someone created a flyer or poster and hung it up in the town hall or post office. This poster would be seen by more people and would spread the news around with more efficiency and complement the word-of-mouth advertising. Then, someone wrote a magazine, a Billboard, and a newspaper. Before you knew it, the Radio came out and it was able to reach people in the immediate area instantly. For people back in the day, the radio was the best thing ever for getting the news out to the people. Then, just when you thought it couldn't get any better than the radio, the Black and White Television came out. Wooooo doggy, Yes, a "black and white Television". Ancient now, I know!

Now, I know some of you may not even know what a black and white television looks like, but it was pretty awesome when it first came out. People were used to hearing music and voices from a small square or rectangle style radio, but to actually see a real person inside of a tube box while you were sitting on your couch in the living room had to be pretty exciting at first. Just look at it like before DSL and Cable Internet, we had "dial up" service and the first version of AOL. That was really great when it first came out, but today, you wouldn't even think about getting a service with a dial up connection. Many people get frustrated if their cell phone service goes from 4G to 2G and are ready to throw their phones away.

Today's televisions have gone to a whole new level. Pretty soon, they won't even need the box frame that the TV shows play in. Everything will be just like a projection television and with today's technology we're almost there. I've seen some test models in the movies where you don't even need a physical box screen for your computers so it's only a matter of time before your television shows will be able to play right in the thin air.

So why am I telling you all of this? It's because marketing your Business has evolved in the same manner. I believe the way to market your business is to focus the majority of your budget towards the Internet and more specifically into Social Media. Social Media is the new "Word of Mouth". It's like traditional word of mouth on steroids. You can reach more people, not only in your local area, but across the whole world and as far as time is concerned, you can advertise and reach people instantly. Yes, with social media, you can gather all of your customers and potential customers in one place and communicate with them at the click of a button. When I say "in one place" I mean on one platform, page, group, or community. You will find that there are many various types of platforms around to build and/or attract your targeted customers and advertise to them at will.

Marketing is another one of those subjects that I can talk about all day. As a matter of fact, I can do a whole course or write a book on marketing to give you more information but at this time, it would take you off of the course that I have planned for you in this book. Just keep in mind that you are going through these particular steps in the book for a reason and you should stay focused on getting yourself set up just as it is written and don't skip any of the steps.

As for the marketing of your business, you can do the basics for now as you are going through these steps, and I will give you some references at the end of this book to help you excel in your marketing skills for your business. One of the things that I wanted to do while writing this book is not to only inform you about the problems, but I wanted to give you some practical solutions for your financial life that you can implement right away.

## Chapter 11

### Time Freedom

Time Freedom! What a great thing! I know this is hard for many people to actually see this for themselves, but it is really possible and can be done in a short amount of time, providing you have followed these steps that I am outlining. Most people don't see this for themselves although they daydream about it happening for them. They daydream and daydream, yet they continue to stay committed to the daily actions that keep them locked into the matrix system.

So, what is Time Freedom?

I'll give you my definition, but I think that it may be different for some people depending on where they are in life. I believe that time freedom is positioning yourself to be able to do whatever you want to do whenever you want to do it. No committed schedules that are not controlled by you. Not having to ask anyone for time off of work. Being able to cancel or schedule appointments, tasks, duties, activities etc.. whenever you want!

When you have time freedom, you can take a week's vacation in Florida and on the seventh day, instantly make a decision to stay an additional two weeks just because you are enjoying yourself. When you have time freedom, you can stay home and watch TV, have fun with your family, volunteer to help children, the elderly or simply just do nothing at all because you are not obligated to be anywhere or to anyone that you can't make adjustments to with a phone call or simply just by making the decision to do or not to do. You'll only have to answer to yourself because you've mastered this game called money by building up enough money and/or having enough passive income coming into your life.

Let's break this down a little. Time Freedom. We have the words "Time" and "Freedom".

**TIME-** What does that look like? Time is the ultimate equalizer because as far as I know, no matter where you are on this earth, no matter what race or ethnic background you claim, we all have the same amount of time. Yes, twenty four hours in a day, seven days a week. Have you ever wondered why some people tend to take time for granted? They always look at life as if they're always going to be here. Keep in mind, we never know how long we're going to be in this life as we know it so, we should all make the best of everyday that we have while giving and getting as much as we can from each day.

So, why is it that some people seem to live this awesome life free of "Time" and a good portion of people accept being confined to allowing someone else to control their time of when they can come and when they can go. Specifically, meaning working at a job. You know, when they tell you that you have to work five days a week from nine to five and you can have two days a week off. Any additional days off, you'll have to ask for permission and/or you'll be allowed to use these specific days called "vacation or sick days". It's not so bad I guess, especially when you're at a job that you enjoy and it's a rewarding service that you provide. Unfortunately, many people are not happy and resent going to their job but never do anything about it. Have you ever wondered why some are accepting of this and some are not? Well, I did. I used to think, why are they doing so much better than us? Why do they have all of these riches? Why are they always on vacation? How did they get these Businesses? How did they get to live in a particular neighborhood and so on....

This was all a mystery to me and there wasn't anyone in my immediate (family, friends or neighborhood area) that could give me an answer to how I could get what these "Time Freedom, rich, successful people" had. Of course, I had plenty of people with opinions and answers with criticism of these successful people, but no answers that were satisfying to me, so I continued on with my search. I continued looking for ways to achieve this lifestyle of the rich and famous as they would call it. Only later in life to find out that the riches were already within me, I just didn't know it or how to tap into it. It's amazing how time can also be a great teacher if you keep your eyes and ears open and are ready to receive.

**FREEDOM**:

Being able to decide what and how you will spend your twenty-four hours per day, not being limited or committed to any portion of your 24 hours and only answering to yourself and/or the creator. It's amazing how so many people just voluntarily give up their FREEDOM of time in exchange for what they think is security, but it's not really secure. When talking about this, I can call on the words of Mr. B. Franklin who said, "Those who give up their FREEDOM for security usually end up getting neither".
For many people, it's a mysterious false sense of security to believe that if they work at a particular JOB for a particular number of years, at the end of that term, they will be taken care of by the JOB or pension that has been accumulated for the rest of their lives. People think that it's the JOB that takes care of them when they retire, when in reality, it's their money that they have been taking out of their paycheck for the past thirty years that's been used to build up their retirement account.

Now that you have a huge chunk of money accumulated for your retirement, they now continue to use your money for their benefit as you are convinced to take monthly allotments of your total pension. While you're taking monthly payments, this gives them more opportunity to continue to re-invest your money and make more profits over and over and over again until you withdraw all of your money.

Upon reaching retirement age with this plan, most people are very surprised to learn that the amount of money that they will be receiving will not be enough for them to live on for the rest of their life, so unfortunately many people end up making one of two decisions. One- They either continue to stay at work, letting go/postponing the idea of retirement or number Two, they retire knowing they will not have enough money to survive and make a decision to pick up another job after retirement. (full time or part time). Both decisions, one and two, eliminates the whole freedom fantasy that was sold to all of us as we entered the workforce at age 18-25.

I know I said that there were two options, but there is one more. Option number Three. That is the option of retiring and not having enough money to do anything. Just barely making it and living month to month, paycheck to paycheck, sitting home every day doing nothing at all. This is very common for many people. They've been so frustrated at their JOB, they're just happy to be leaving the workplace and they'll settle for just being away from there. All in all, the old saying of living it up and enjoying the Golden Years are not as golden as they make it sound when you are just starting your job at age 25.

**Chapter #12**

**Step 9   Making your freedom plan
The 60/40 formula**

Ok, here we go with the 60/40 plan.  I purposely saved this towards the end and had you go through all of the other steps in order to prepare you for this process.  Hopefully, you've been a good student and have taken all of the steps before this so that you will be able to receive this 60/40 plan with an open mind.  Warning! If you have cheated and skipped through, you'll only be hurting your own mental state of understanding and will most likely not get it or end up quitting because you are not fully prepared.  So, If you did cheat, I encourage you to go back, start over and implement all of the steps up to this point.

Ok, now that you have gone through all of the steps, I want you to think about where you received your money management skills from.  Most people receive their philosophy from their parents, misinformed bank customer service reps, mortgage reps, real estate agents, financial brokers, stockbrokers, and so on, most of whom have a financial interest in keeping you in debt or being able to use your money for their benefit.  I point this out because for the majority of people, these people and institutions affect where the majority of your money is spent once you earn it.  This is why it is important for you to understand the ROI concept that we spoke about earlier.  Knowing your ROI and understanding that you are the most important asset is key to growing your money and then having your money work for you.  As always, I'd like to give you some examples of what I'm speaking about to help you get a vision and be able to understand.  It would be easy to just give you the "What" or "How to" with the 60/40 plan, but that would be a disservice to you as most of you will probably miss the "Why"..  It is the "Why" that will help you carry this to the end for both you and your family.

Let's start with the concept of placing your money in the bank. Have you ever noticed that in many towns, there are tons and tons of Banks all around? It's really like an overkill. In some downtown areas, it seems like there is a Bank on every corner. Have you ever asked yourself why? Don't feel bad if you haven't because most people never thought about it. It's been so embedded in us all that we just assume that we should be surrounded by the Banks. So why do they surround us like this? Why are they all over the place? Basically, it's so that we can be conditioned to have easy access to place our money into their care. What's in it for us? Well, we're conditioned to think that our money is safe and that our money will be able to grow with interest by placing it in the Bank, but it is only a false sense of security. In reality, our money is not safe at all and we're definitely not seeing our money grow.

What's in it for them? Well, they have the luxury and pleasure of being able to receive our money as we place our money with them for holding or investing. Now they are in control. Initially, the Banks don't really have tons of money, it's a paper illusion.

In addition to holding our money, they also are given several opportunities to make money off of our money while it is placed in the bank. Did you know that for every dollar that we give the Bank, they're allowed to borrow up to nine times that amount of money to use for other banking services, like car loans, mortgages, personal loans, etc...?
Yup, that's what's happening. These loans that we apply for at the Bank are loans based off of other people's money. (People just like you and I)
This cycle continues on and on, year after year for generations and most people don't even realize this is happening and furthermore, many people don't realize the damage that this cycle has on individuals and their entire family's financial future.

Now if you're just hearing about this for the first time, don't feel too bad. This type of information is purposefully kept away from the general public. They really don't want you to know. On the other hand, there are some of us that accidentally stumble upon this information about the banks and this concept of keeping us locked in the cycle of dependence, poor man's mentality and financially enslaved to the system. Unfortunately, the worst part is that even after being exposed or enlightened to this information, many people either deny that the system is like this and/or they just simply continue "as they were", before learning about this information. That my friend is the tragic part. Which one will you be?

**"KNOWING IS ONLY THE BEGINNING"**

I remember watching the movie "The Matrix" when Morpheus enlightened Neo to the real reality and then gave him the option of continuing to learn more of the truth or going back to the Matrix and being like everyone else. The Red Pill or the Blue Pill, which one do you choose? Believe it or not, we face that decision in life more times than people realize. There are many times in our lives when we are exposed to something, and we get that feeling that it's not quite right. "Something is different or something is wrong" "Have I been doing this wrong all of this time?" After that feeling, we make a conscious or unconscious decision to change or continue on the same path, even when we feel something is not right.
Today you will be having your choice of the Blue Pill or Red Pill...

Now, if you continue on your financial path with no clear plan in mind, you will end up like the average American. You may end up retired, maybe with a pension plan or not, and maybe collecting social security or not, whereas we're not sure how long that will be around. This keeps you right on the edge of being broke and/or homeless just like when you were working for the past 30 years. Yes, the average worker and retired person are just that close to being homeless. They say that most people are only a few months or paychecks away from being homeless or broke.

Today is a new day!   Now that you've set yourself up and positioned yourself for success, you can now be on your way to mastering this game called money.   Let's look at some numbers again.  Here is the basic formula that I would like for you to implement into your financial life.  Of course, it's not ingrained in stone, it's for you to use as a blueprint.  I highly recommend using it "as is" in the beginning to use as structure for yourself.  This will be keeping things simple. The simple way is usually the best, most direct, way. Keep in mind that if you're an employee, we're going to be talking about after tax money, meaning your "Net" or "your take home amount".  When talking money with industry people like banking, finance & the mortgage industry, they tend to use your "Gross" income when doing calculations.  I don't understand why they insist on doing this because, the bottom line is, you do not live off of your gross income, you live off of your net income, so this is what we'll be working with.

So upon receiving your net income, I want you to start to separate your money the following way.

**10%  Give!**

Give to who, you may ask?  Well, that's going to be on each individual.  To some this may mean Tithing, to others it may mean giving to someone in need.  Maybe giving to an organization, a person, a school, a soup kitchen, Hospital, creating a scholarship, or anything with the act of doing for someone else besides yourself.   You can even perform random acts such as being at a grocery store and paying for the tab for the person in front of or behind you.  One year, we purchased some grocery store gift cards and randomly passed them out to customers in the store while they were shopping.

You can imagine the looks on some of their faces when we did this. Some were filled with joy and others had looks of doubt, looking for the catch, thinking we were going to ask them for something or as if the gift cards were not real. All in all, it's a great thing to do and it's rewarding to watch their expressions of Joy. You'll be surprised how much ten, twenty, fifty or one hundred dollars could affect someone's life.

## 10 % Long Term Retirement Investment

Traditionally for most people, this is being done with their pension plan. The JOB will take a certain portion of your paycheck and place it in your retirement fund. Remember this is part of your Gross income when your JOB is taking out for your pension. What we'll be doing is working from your net income. So yes, if it looks like you'll be having a second pension plan, then you're right, you will be having a second pension plan. The difference will be, with this long term pension plan you'll be in control and not some big giant company that doesn't have any real interest in your financial freedom, only theirs. At the end of the day, once you know how to do it, no one is going to take a better interest in YOU, better than you.

Now with this 10% investment for your long term, you must always remember that this is for you and/or your family for long term goals only. This is not something for you to accumulate several thousands and then use to remodel your kitchen, go on vacation or buy a car. NO! It's not that type of savings. We'll touch on that in a little bit. This long-term investment is strictly for when you stop working your JOB at the standard retirement age of 65 or when you reach the vision for your ultimate early retirement age which can be prior to 65, whichever comes first. Some people would like to retire at age 35, 40, 50. It varies with some people. There are some professions when you can complete twenty-five or thirty years of service and officially retire and still not be 65 years of age yet.

Remember, do not let anything or any person take you off of this plan. If you seriously value your future YOU, then I strongly encourage you to stick to this part of the plan without any interruptions.

As I am writing this, I may or may not have spoken to you about the power of compounding interest. If so, make sure you go over that section again and truly understand it because compounding is one of the key components to your accumulation of money and your retirement. Just to give you an example, let's say you were earning approximately $2,000 take home (net) every month. Remember, we deal with net income, not gross income. If you invested $200 per month, every month from age 25 to the retirement age of 65 at 7%, that would be approximately $534,024 accumulated. Now that grand total is using a total investment of $2,500 per year, so you will have to add in an additional $100 a year to make that work because your $200 per month totals up to $2,400 per year, but I was using this as an example to keep the numbers whole and simple. For your viewing, Maybe I'll place a couple of sample charts with different tables for you to use as a reference. If you're anything like me, sometimes when reading something, I may or may not get it right away, but when I see a picture, it becomes much clearer for me. I'm guessing that there will be some readers of this book that are just like me. Also keep in mind that this accumulated amount of $534,024 is extra. You'll still have your pension and your equalizing balancing secondary social security plan if it's still around. Now where getting somewhere! This should take care of you during your retirement years so you are not in a position where you have to go out and get a job or start a second career to keep up with your current lifestyle.

Unfortunately, so many people have fallen into this trap of having to continue to work after doing twenty-five to thirty years on a job. It's really not fair, but most of us have been programmed to be consumers and not financially prepared for retirement. They think that their employer's financial plan will take care of them and by the time most people realize it's not so, it's too late.

Just like in some of the previous chapters I have placed some reference links for you to be able to visit and create your own numbers where you can mix and match to build your personal retirement plan and chart your own retirement plan course. *Ref links and Pics on my website.

## 10%  Investing for NOW!

With this 10%, you'll be using it for investment for right now, real time investments.  You'll be using this to purchase inventory, tools, programs, Books, start a business, real estate, tickets for events and most importantly, things that revolve around YOU because you are the most important investment.  With that said, you must spend as much of this money as you can to improve your technical skills, sales skills, people skills, financial skills, etc.  Always remember that statement about YOU being the most important INVESTMENT.  With that said, that means that YOU are responsible for making sure that the things that you spend this 10% of your money on brings back a return on your money. (Your ROI)  The ultimate goal is for that return to be monetary, but not necessarily so all of the time.  Sometimes, the return can be in personal growth within YOU initially and then later convert to a monetary value, but it should always be some sort of forward movement.  One of the worse things that I've seen is when someone takes in a ton of knowledge, maybe spend a great deal of money to learn something and then never implement anything.  They just become one of the great knowers in life.  They know a little bit about everything.  They know and know and know and know, but never do anything because they know so much. (haha)  Have you ever known anyone like that?  I think that most of us have a friend or family member that fits that description.  At least one in your family or maybe even at your JOB.  Now  if you are searching for that person within your friends, family or workplace and can't find them, then look out because that person just might YOU.  Scary, huh?

Let me give you some examples of what you can do with your 10% INVESTMENT for now Money. In order to keep things simple, we're going to use the same numbers of $2000 per month just like in the long-term investment section. After all, they're both 10% of which we have $200 to work with each month.

Now if you remember from an earlier chapter, I gave an example of a business that you could start at home that would cost you fifty dollars per month to start. Using that as a reference, if you have two hundred dollars per month to invest in yourself, then with that business of fifty dollars per month, you are now left with one hundred and fifty dollars of INVESTMENT Now Money for the month. Your first priority is to capitalize on that fifty dollars that you are spending and to get that fifty dollars to the point of which the business pays you back a minimum of fifty dollars on a monthly basis. So as in the case that I used previously, it took four recurring sales to get a monthly income of $60. (That's $15 each sale) So your goal is to get to a minimum of four sales as quickly as possible. Meanwhile, you have $150 of your $200 left. What do you do with this money? Well this is going to depend on where you are in life. Example, if you a shy person and do not have any people skills or sales skills, then I would suggest you start to use some of that money to invest in building YOU, specifically in this case, building your sales and people skills. The reason is because in most businesses people are at the root of you making money because you will ultimately want them to buy something from you.

Now don't feel bad about this. Sometimes when people hear "Buy something" or "Sell something", they clam up. Some people have this mental block about selling something to others as if it's going make them look like they're a bad person, so they shy away. "Oh no, I don't want to do sales." I hear this pretty often. In fact, most people, maybe even everyone, are selling something in one way or another. People sell their morals or belief system to convince people how they are or how they want to be perceived all of the time.

Some people use their morals or belief system to convince people to follow them. What about the people that use their morals, belief system, or behaviors to persuade other people to be their friend. hmmm Have you ever thought about the selling process that a person goes through when they get dressed for the day? The clothes they put on, the shoes they wear, the cologne or perfume that they put on. What do you think about when you are deciding what to wear for the day? What about the words that one person says to another during a first meeting and even after knowing each other for a long period of time. Have you ever thought about the words, actions, the physical, emotional and verbal actions that a person uses that are merely actions of the average salesperson.

Yes, everybody is selling something at some point in their life. Some for the good and some may not be for good reasons, but we all have intentions within our actions. So, my wish for you is to recognize this in yourself and learn how to improve your sales skills and learn how to direct your skills to be of value to other people so much to the point of which they will want to pay you for solving a problem or giving them solutions to situations that they may have in their life.

On the other hand, if you are a person that's already comfortable with yourself and comfortable with the word "Sales", I would still put some focus on personal growth and in addition, I would focus on finding ways to systematize and automate as many of the little tasks that are not of great value of your time. Meaning daily tasks like checking emails, sending out emails, doing social media post, building Ad's, writing articles or Post, etc. These things should be either outsourced or limited to one or two days per week. The other 3 or 5 days should be spent building your business, your system and making sales.

I suggest that if you have the skills for selling and talking with people, then you should focus on getting the sales during the majority of your time. Meaning "closing them or getting them to buy your product or service". Example- Phone calls, Facebook Chats, instant messages, podcast, seminars, webinars, Scopes, one on one appointments, and so on.

Let the Post, Tweets, Pings, Articles, Blog, Videos, emails and other marketing material reach them, provide value to and attract them to you and you focus on closing the deal. Do the things that you are stronger at and that will put more money into your business faster. You must focus on getting your first four recurring sales as fast as possible, so you will be able to take your $50 a month business from a liability to now being an asset. Even if it's only a five or ten percent growth. The whole point is to get your ROI in a positive cash flow position.

Investing now is for building now. Investing long term is for your retirement at your desired age, so when you're investing for now, your goal is to get your money to turn over as quickly as possible. You want to get your money in the position where it is earning you money instead of you simply paying out to everyone each month. Investing NOW is about building a business that will add additional income for you to combine with your income from your JOB if you have one. This way, as you grow your business, you'll want to get to a point where you can add an additional 10% or more of your earnings into your "Investment for Long Term Fund". This money may even be in another investment platform specifically designed for your business that will give you additional tax benefits. The main point will be to start re-investing your profits into your future. You can start with adding an additional 10% to your long-term account, then use the rest to re-invest in your "Investing now Business" and scale up.

You can scale up your Traffic and Marketing to help give you more exposure to more potential customers. You can also use this extra money to outsource or automate more of your daily, weekly or monthly tasks.

As your part time business begins to grow, try not to lose sight of your original retirement goal. Particularly if you have a full time JOB. I say this because sometimes when someone starts a part time business and they get a little momentum going in the beginning, they get the notion that they do not have to continue working their full time JOB and quit too early to pursue the part time business thinking they that if they were doing it full time, they will be able to make twice the amount of money or more.

Not necessarily the case. In many cases, people find themselves with too much time on their hands and tend to not execute as well as they did while working their full time JOB. In other cases, some people find themselves in a situation where now their formal part time business income is now their full-time income. At first quitting may appear to be a great thing until you realize that you have just positioned yourself to be dependent on your part time business income for both your business and your personal monthly expenses. Now, you've lost your leverage! You've taken away, unknowingly, the leverage that you had in order to reach your early retirement goal as quickly as you had intended.

Before you quit your JOB, remember a few things. Again, first remember your original plan for your retirement. The amount of money that you wanted to accumulate, the time period of when you wanted to retire and the lifestyle that you want to live when you retire. These things should always be stored in your brain and used as the foundation of your decisions. Next, remember that many businesses fail within the first 5-10 years, mainly due to "Revenue vs Expenses".

Yes, they get tapped out just like MMA, having to carry the expenses of the business for so long and not making enough profit. So with that in mind, hopefully, you've followed our model of utilizing the internet as a possible system for your business which can cut down the expenses by a huge percentage. Another thing to consider before quitting your JOB, is to make sure that you are making more money in your part time business annually than at your full time JOB. Don't just react to you having a good month in your business or executing one deal that landed you a big paycheck. Then you say, "oh if I can do this part time, just think what I can do if I wasn't at my JOB". That's one of the major mistakes people make. I like to look at it another way. "If I could make this big commission paycheck part time while working at my full time JOB, I wonder how much more I can make doing this part time while working at my JOB."

This is where you want to be! Now we're talking real retirement planning. Just think, If you set yourself up as described in the beginning and followed the 60/40 plan, all of this income coming into your business is extra money. Think about all of the great vacations you can have, people you can help, and also think about the extra contributions to your retirement account you can make. Now with using the retirement chart from earlier, you can accelerate your retirement date and/or increase the amount that you accumulate for your original date. Both outcomes are great, but only if you stick to the plan and work both your JOB and your part time business. Do not forget your original retirement accumulation goal and passive formula.

Now, as always, there are exceptions! Generally speaking, if my part time business was doing so well that it exceeded my full-time income in one year that would definitely raise my eyebrows and cause me to take a closer look at what was happening. With all cases being different and depending on a person's JOB, whether they just are totally unhappy there, the number of years they have in, the individual age, and other factors to consider.

In general, when I hit the point of matching or exceeding my full-time job's income with my part time business income, I would then do a test by shifting the amount of my expenses and seeing if my business could carry them for the whole year or two, bringing in money on a bi-weekly or monthly basis. While still working at my JOB, I would then save/invest all of the income from my full time JOB. Yes, every paycheck. I would save/invest it as if I didn't have it coming in just to make sure that I can survive full time off my business income, and not just be living commission to commission to pay my bills, I would expect to be making over and beyond that of which I need to live off of.

What would be the point of leaving the JOB to struggle in the business from commission to commission? "None at all!" That will be pushing yourself backward and have you end up in the same place as the rest of the ninety five percent except you're struggling with your business to stay broke versus struggling and staying broke on a JOB. Commission to commission or paycheck to paycheck, ultimately, it's the same thing.

I want you to imagine the feeling that you would have working at your JOB knowing that you do not need the paychecks that you pick up every week. Imagine how it would feel to have all of your bills being paid by your part time business while you are saving/investing all of your money from your JOB. Imagine your attitude while working at your JOB. You'll probably have a whole different pep in your step. Imagine the multiple streams of income opportunities that you'll be able to have because of your strong foundation and not to mention the additional assets that you would be able to purchase as funding from various lending institutions will reach out and be available to you.

One of the great things about having money is that it attracts money, you will find that by saving and investing your money to the point where you accumulate thousands and hundreds of thousands, you'll also increase your purchasing power. Purchasing power increases your ability to have your money to work for you and make more money on your behalf.

### 5% Misc Short Term, Emergency Fund

Setting up this 5% portion of the formula may not seem like much in the beginning. This is probably why so many people tend not to do this part in life. It seems like a small amount, but it can play a big part in the outcome of your plan. If I could describe this part of your plan in any manner, I would choose the saying "Murphy's Law". Yes, Murphy's law is bound to happen. No matter how well you plan things out, no matter how good of a job you have, no matter how great your new part time business is, something is bound to happen and throw a wrench in the plan.

The major questions are almost always, 1. Are you prepared for it? And 2. What are you going to do about it? Both of these have probably hit home to you in at least one aspect of your life and one thing that appears to be consistent with many people is that most people are not prepared for miscellaneous mishaps that sneak up in their lives. Many people do not have an emergency fund available to draw from when unexpected financial situations come up. So the next question of "What are you going to do about it?" is just as damaging if not more than the first question. As stated, many people don't prepare for financial emergencies, so when they happen, it becomes a breaking point for the majority of people. It is said that most people are only a few paychecks away from being homeless.

Now I know that sounds harsh and in reality, it wouldn't happen in a few checks, but it would definitely be the beginning of a downhill ride for many people getting behind on rent, mortgage, bills and so on. Once you get behind on the first month, it can turn into a domino effect and financially, mentally and physically destroy a person to the point of no return. So, the question of "what are you going to do about it?" remains in the hands of each individual and their belief. They have a choice to focus on miscellaneous acts that occur in all of our lives and let it consume them or recognize what has happened and seek out an alternative solution for getting through the situation.

I know you may be saying, it's not that simple. My answer to that statement is, "it is, if you think it is", meaning it can be that simple if you believe it's that simple. On the other hand, if you don't believe it's that simple, then you will be programming your mind to think that it's difficult. You see, your mind is going to do exactly what you tell it to do. If you think negatively, think you can't make it, think you can't do it, or think it won't work, your mind will gladly support that for you. On the other hand, if you think positively and think that you can do it, there is a solution, think, you can make it, or think you will make it, your mind will gladly support that for you. Remember your brain is your central processing unit. You cannot go beyond the limits of which you think.

With all of that said, start up your 5% fund to prepare yourself for an emergency and make sure that you define what an emergency is. This is not a dipping fund for you to use on a regular basis. Emergencies only! Think about the past and try to remember the things that happened that just blew your budget away. Can you remember a time when things were going fairly well and out of the blue, your transmission went out, you had to get new tires, your heater stopped working in the winter, etc. Write out some things that are real emergencies that have to be done right away and will not be able to wait until next month or your next bonus check. I'd like to suggest to you to please be reasonable and very clear on what an emergency is. Make sure that you write down some of these expected or should I say unexpected emergencies, so that you can get a picture in your mind of what a real emergency looks like.

Again, remember ladies a real emergency does not look like that "spectacular two day sale" on a dress or some nice pumps. The same goes for the guys. Just because the latest "going to be a classic" version of a sneaker is about to be released or the fourth maybe the fifth version of that video game is coming out, does not make it an excuse to tap into this emergency fund. As you can see, I'm having fun with this part, but you know that it's real.

You have saved up seven hundred dollars or maybe a couple thousands of dollars and you figure "oh, I'll just borrow from this 5% emergency fund, I'll put it back" Stop!!! Don't do that! It's only the beginning of a downhill ride to your emergency fund disappearing. Ask me how I know......(Been there, Done that!!)

### 5% Marketing Promotions

Marketing and Promotions is a vital part of your business and life in general. When I think of marketing and promotions, I think of "sales". I know this is a scary word for many people because again for many people when they think of sales, they think about the pushy car salesman or nerdy Insurance salesman that comes around knocking door to door. They also think about the annoying telemarketer that calls your house while you're eating dinner, the desperate retail salesperson that jumps at you to get a sale as soon as you walk in the store. While some of these may or may not be true, try not to look at it in that manner. I like to say that everyone is selling something, and everyone is self-made.

The thing is most people either don't realize it or are not honest enough with themselves to know this. Think about this, everyone is selling something. Think about the simplest thing like friendship. When two people meet for the very first time, they are either selling themselves so that the other person may like them or selling a bad message so the other person may not like them. Either way, you are selling a message. Teenagers and adults do it every day when thinking about what they should wear for the day. Women and men ask these questions all of the time "How will this look on me?" "How do I look?" "What do you think?" "Should I wear this?" "Do you like these shoes?". These same type of questions can also be applied to one's personality when you are trying to figure out "if someone is a nice person?", "Will we get along?", "Do you like the way I look?", "I like the way we get along", Can we be friends?, and the ultimate "Will you marry me?"

Of course, I can go on and on with these types of questions, but the main question I'd like to ask you is "why do you think we ask these questions to others?" and/or at a minimum to ourselves. These types of questions are all part of our personal promotions bucket where we are attempting to sell/market our personality, our looks, our style, our personal service, our beliefs, our life to another person or group of people. It's happening all of the time. Again, friendships, acquaintances, coworkers, business partners, boyfriend, girlfriend, husband, wife, children, siblings, we're all selling. So why does it change when it comes to selling/marketing a product or starting a business? It's all in your mind. Take that negative image of selling out of your mind and know that if you have a good business or product that's good for people, you should do whatever promotions and marketing that you have to do to get your targeted customer to buy your product.

At the end of the day, Marketing is the key to growing your business. If you show me a business that's not marketing, I'll show you a business that's on its way out of business. In today's society, one of the keys to marketing is using the Internet. I believe that it's a must to learn how to market on the internet and if you don't have the time to learn, you should have someone on your staff or hire someone to do this. I believe newspapers and magazine ads will soon be a thing of the past. Word of mouth is still good if you have a responsive group of customers and you are mainly looking to keep your business local, however, word of mouth can be the slow way to go, unless you combine the internet with it which emphasizes my point. The internet is the way to go for sure. Imagine having a social media presence where your customers can continually be updated on what's happening with your company. Imagine customers at your business making a purchase and they check in with their social media platform to let everyone know that they are there at your place.

Now that's instant free advertising. Letting all of their friends and followers know about your place gives you credibility and also can attract people to your social media page and/or even better have someone make a decision to immediately go to your business that very day. That's word of mouth squared to the 10th power.

In addition to your current customers spreading the word about your business, you also have the power of advertising to new potential customers. Advertising online is without a doubt the most cost-effective way to reach your current and potential customers. As a comparison, think about this. With traditional newspaper advertising, when you place an ad, it reaches everyone that purchases that paper for the day. Some may be interested in your type of business, and some may not have any interest at all in your type of business. Needless to say, after reading the paper for that day, your ad is gone. You have no way of telling if you've reached your targeted customer or not. Your only recourse is to wait and see if anyone comes into your business and mentions the ad that you placed. Here you have a one-day ad, and you still have to wait and see if you've reached any of your targeted customers and you've probably paid a couple hundred dollars for your ad to have been placed. Most people will not re-read the same paper later in the day or the next day. In general, most people get rid of their paper after reading it. On the other hand, when advertising on the internet, you have the ability to get in front of your targeted market instantly. Targeted Market: Meaning, people that are actually interested in the type of business or products that you have. In addition to getting in front of the right people, you can also set yourself up so that you can be in front of them multiple times per day and/or several days in the future, all for a price that would be a lot less than placing an Ad in your local newspaper.

These internet placed ads can reach your customers on their desktops, laptops and mobile devices. You can be with them wherever they go.

This is why I strongly suggest that you have someone on your team or staff that can implement this form of marketing for your business. Hire someone to do this task if you have too, but make sure that this is a must. Then as your marketing efforts get great returns, you can scale it up to get more customers and to re-service your present customers. Always take care of your current customers. Have coupons, frequent visitor cards, referral rewards, a customer appreciation day, etc. It's less expensive to market to your current customers and easier to get a current customer to buy again than to get a new prospect to buy.

So, this type of marketing is a must for longevity. First market to get customers then you market to service your current customers while continuing to market for new customers.

In the beginning, you'll be starting off with a small budget for marketing, but keep in mind that this is definitely an area that you should increase in the future. For now, just to make sure that you track your marketing budget, so you do not overspend and then re-invest any of the profits back into your marketing. Also keep in mind that this 5% is from your personal (Job) income. When you start to make money with your part-time business, you can also take 5% or more to use for marketing. For now, take advantage of all of the free marketing that you can and gather your customers and potential customers on social media and/or to your home base meaning your website/blog and your email marketing platform.

We can talk more about marketing at a later time.

## 60%  Your foundation, personal expenses, and wants

Here we go!  Now depending on where you are in life, meaning age, financial stability, belief, and so on, this 60% may be too much for some and it may not be enough for others.  With that said, I ask that you refer to the beginning of this book where I spoke about getting yourself set up for receiving this.  So, if you've set your lifestyle and finances up as I spoke of in the beginning, then this will fit right in and you should feel very comfortable with these proportions of your money.  If not, then you'll have to make some adjustments until you can get yourself in a position to do this.

Always remember that this is your (living now) foundation.  This 60% plan is only the beginning of your financial freedom formula.  When writing this blueprint out, I tried to keep the average person in mind.  I wanted this to be something that any working person can do regardless of their profession.  Many people have been convinced that being in certain professions are the only way to be able to obtain financial freedom for themselves.  That is so far from the truth.  This is why the book is set up like this to give the "Average Joe" the ability to live financially free and/or at a minimum be able to retire and live the lifestyle that they are currently living or better.  One of the things that I really don't like to see is when someone is at retirement age and they will not retire simply because they will not be able to retire and have all of their expenses paid.  The Awakening!  It's like the Matrix System is real.  Teaching the majority of people to follow this system that keeps them trapped and enslaved by circulating them through the controlled school system until high school.  After high school, if you are to be so lucky, you get to go to college where you get to give the matrix more money by way of a college tuition to support the cause.

Once you are complete with college, you are honored to be able to enter the workforce where you can get a JOB, pay off your tuition and work for the rest of your life. Well, they say until retirement, but for many, it becomes the rest of their lives. This is why it is important for you to focus on a plan for yourself because you are the only one that can do the absolute best job for YOU. I encourage you not to buy into the propaganda of the Media, Hollywood, Politicians and so on. The Education SYSTEM and big plan of going to school, get a job, pay your bills and retire, does not work for the benefit of the majority.

I encourage you not to buy into the propaganda that we should live in fear, struggle, be poor and dependent upon our government to make our lives better, especially when it's them who have created and still creating these situations.

Does it really make sense to depend on the system that created the problem to get you out? It does not benefit them, so why would they want to save you? They will only string you along enough for them to accomplish their goals, meanwhile leaving you with living in fear and struggling for the rest of your life, generation after generation. You must take charge of your own financial destiny! It's the only way you can make the change. Make the change from we the people, to me and my family or as I like to say, "me and my people". If more people started to take care of their own personal finances, it would make our economy much more secure. It can get the government and big companies out of your pocket and free you from their dependence.

Without a doubt in many ways, we live in a wonderful country with a lot of good qualities about her, while at the same time, there is a certain group or groups of people that have made this same country unbearable for many that live here and also harmed others outside of our country. Nonetheless, we have to learn how to figure our way around all of the madness and look for the good and utilize the resources and laws that are already in place to make a living here in this county better for ourselves and others.

Now to the 60%. If you have done things according to the blueprint that I laid out, you should be able to pay for all of your monthly home expenses and wants with 60% of your income. Remember, this does not include any of your part time business income. This is only in reference to your income from your full time Job.
60% should be able to pay your rent or mortgage, gas & electricity, water, car note if any, transportation expenses, food, clothing, and so on.

Now here is a sample of someone with a working salary of $25, 000 per year. Let's say that after taxes, you bring home approximately $1,500 per month. 60% of the $1500 would be $900. This means that the above items cannot go over $900 per month. i.e. rent, gas & electricity, water, car, transportation, etc.... Once you break this rule, it's very hard to reset and start over, so make sure that you start from the beginning doing the right thing. If you are making $50,000 per year, then of course the numbers would double to $3000 per month take home and 60% of that would be $1800 per month that you can use for rent/mortgage, gas/electric, water, car, transportation, etc...

This 60% is set up like this for a good reason. The one thing that you do not want to do is to expense yourself out like many people do. Many people look at their net income and automatically start to expense and excuse their way through their money. They have been conditioned to charge, swipe or purchase everything that they feel they can cover with the amount of their paycheck. I believe it's instilled in most of us by our education system and advertising.

What's my take home, they think. Ok $1500 per month, so I can pay rent for about $1000, utilities 150, car note $300, and I'll make it through until the next pay with the remaining $50 or play the Peter and Paul game until they get a part time job or a raise. That's the thinking at least. In reality it doesn't work out and many people continue to play that game month after month, year after year until "Murphy's Law" kicks in and something goes wrong. The car breaks down, you get laid off from work, rent goes up, etc... It's bound to happen, so why not be prepared and start yourself a 5% fund to prepare yourself just like I mentioned earlier in the book. It's a win win for you. If something happens, then you're prepared and if nothing goes wrong, then you've created yourself an additional savings/investment fund on the side. I know some of you may be thinking that because you make more than $1500 per month, that this does not apply to you.

Well, the ratios are pretty similar with people that earn $3,000, $5,000, $10,000 or more per month. It's not the amount of money that you make, it's the way that you think about money and what you do with it once you get it. Without getting into specifics, there are people in the television, movie, sports and entertainment business that go through the same process.

You hear about it all of the time, when a well-known actor or athlete is homeless, broke or filing for bankruptcy and you scratch your head and wonder "why?". This is the reason. They somehow expensed themselves out and purchased more than their income or contract could handle. Income from Contracts, JOB Paychecks, Business Income/Commissions, it's all the same and can all be wasted away in the same manner regardless of the amount. This is even more so when it's earned income, but it happens with passive income from business as well.

Now back to us average folks. Let this be your plan. If you have followed me and set yourself up from the beginning of this book, then this will be hard, but manageable. On the other hand, if you have skipped through to get to this section, you'll probably think that I'm crazy or that this is impossible to do. Nonetheless, you'll have to find a way to get started with some version of this formula. I believe that most people have already expensed themselves to the point where this formula will appear to be impossible to do, but I'd like to encourage you to take a serious look at where you are in life and what it is that you want to accomplish in life, and after you do that, I'd like you to ask yourself this question. "Is what I'm doing right now, taking me to where I want to be?". Meaning, the money that I have coming in, the people that I am serving, the way I manage my money, is my money working for me or am I just working and chasing the money?

Talk to yourself and be honest with yourself because it's easy to lie and give a perfect answer to someone else, but at the end of the day, you have to live with that lie, you have to live with the results that you have. Being broke is a mindset that will keep you living paycheck to paycheck and justifying it. So where do you want to be? How many years do you want to get there (1, 5, 10 years)? What would this do for you when you achieve this goal? Remember the Benefit of the Benefit. Who else will this serve by you obtaining your goals? What will change by you obtaining your goals?

Now for the big question. So what are you going to do about it?

Mastering this game called money is more than learning some information, learning a formula and thinking you got this or, oh, I already know this. It's about taking massive, massive action. It's about not being afraid to do the things that are going to place you in position for you to WIN. You can't be afraid of the changes. Well, you can be afraid, but you must face the changes. You can't be worried about what others may think of you. What if you have to make changes that would change the car that you drive or change the place where you live?

What if it means that you have to go from living in a house to moving into an apartment or condo? What if it means that you may have to move back home with your parents or move in with your children? Are you prepared to make that decision in order to win this money game and gain your financial FREEDOM?

How much are you willing to change for you to WIN? I do realize that this will be hard for many people. Again, I suspect that most people have not positioned themselves to be able to do this plan comfortably right away and they WILL have to make some changes. It all comes down to   HOW BAD DO YOU WANT IT?

Try it my way, make the necessary sacrifices that you need to do to get yourself in play with mastering this game called money.  You'll be surprised at what you can do when you put your mind to it and you'll be oh so happy when you reach your goal and master this game called money.

Mastering this game called money is not as difficult as it may seem. It's really about building up your passive income enough to carry your expenses, which should include your wants and needs. That in itself is the formula.

"When your passive income exceeds your expenses, you are technically FINANCIALLY FREE. Plain and simple! I believe that many people think that they have to be wealthy to be financially free. Meaning, having a particular amount of money in the millions or billions. This is not necessarily so. Again, you just have to reach the point where your passive income exceeds your expenses. Now your income is supporting you!

For the most part you have 3 ways of getting to this point.

Option #1. You can work at a job for 30-45 years and retire with a pension. Note: This pension is now passive income, because it comes to you every month without you no longer having to report to work. On the downside, in today's society, the pension may not be enough, and it may not even be there after you put in your 30-45 years. Also, the other downside is the amount of time that it takes for you to obtain this form of passive income. 30- 45 years is a long time to obtain this goal.

Option #2. You can try to save up enough money that would pay you monthly dividends that exceed your monthly expenses and you could be financially free. Meaning if your expenses were $3000 per month, like in our previous examples, you'll need at least $300,000 to live off of a 10% return on your money. Not considering any misc fees involved. The only issue is, today, many people living with expenses of $3000 per month usually have a net income close to $3000 per month or less and are expensed out. So, how would they be able to save enough money? Most people will not be able to do this, therefore this option would be void for many people. Once someone gets expensed out, it's hard for them to be able to save anything, especially $300,000.

3. Option #3. You can do as recommended throughout this book and set yourself up with a part time business while combining the 60/40 plan and follow the steps as outlined. At the end of the day, you only have to answer to YOU. Regardless of what I suggest, and any other writers or readers may say, you're going to be the one that makes the decision for you and your family. You have to live with the decisions, good or bad, but you should also consider the fact that if you are one that has children, it is a huge chance that your children will fall into the same financial plan that you have. So, if you continue to live paycheck to paycheck, I can almost guarantee you that subconsciously the same pattern will be passed down to your children.

If you doubt what I am saying, then take a close look at yourself, be honest and then look at your parents and measure how financially close you are to them.
It seems to be across the board for many of us, regardless of our Race or Ethnicity, we tend to follow the patterns of our parents financially. Yes, there are exceptions, but for the most part it is a continuum from generation to generation. Let's have you be the one that break the chains of the financial slavery and help save the generations to come both in your family and others. Don't just do this for yourself, once you obtain your financial FREEDOM status, you should be happy and ecstatic about sharing what you've accomplished and teach others how they can be financially free also.

Now I'm going to let you in on a little secret and if you were really paying attention throughout this book, then you would've noticed that our plan, which is option #3 actually uses a combination of all three of the options. The difference is the way I have it set up. It accelerates your FINANCIAL FREEDOM. It' helps you Master This Game Called Money in a shorter time period than it would take working 30-45 years or taking 30 years to save up $300,000.

So again, I strongly encourage you to try out my blueprint. Implement this in your life for six months or a year and see the difference. You'll be surprised how much you can do once you follow the blueprint and see what you accomplish in a year's time.

For your convenience, I placed a reference site at the end for you to use to get information for setting up a part time business and implementing this plan for your life and to help you get on track to mastering your money and obtaining financial freedom. Visit my page and also reach out to me on social media.

## FINANCIAL FREEDOM

Remember financial freedom does not necessarily mean that you have millions or even billions of dollars. This is part of the confusion of many people. Being financially FREE simply means that when your monthly passive income exceeds your monthly expenses, you have now created financial freedom for yourself. Notice, I did not mention any particular amount of money or net worth. I'm only talking about the amount of money that comes into your life each month on a passive basis versus the amount of money that must be paid out each month. (Expenses) Everyone can do this, regardless of their profession. It's not about the amount of money that you make on your JOB. (That's Earned Income) It's not about your titled profession. It's not about how many degrees that you have from college. (That's an illusion) It's all about the numbers and the numbers are plain, simple and to the point. Don't let other people make it into a complicated formula by telling you that you have to be in a particular profession or have a certain degree to obtain financial freedom. That's what people are conditioned to think. They're taught that "you have to have a degree if you want to be somebody". Getting your degree does not make you financially free. More false teachings being instilled in the people.

Finally, you can do this by working on a JOB for 30 plus years, anticipate what your pension from your JOB is going to be, then make sure that your monthly expenses are well below that amount, and you can then be financially free. Note: (You should keep inflation in mind when you do it this way. Most JOB pension yearly increments may or may not keep up with inflation and therefore, if your pension is just barely over your monthly expenses, you will eventually be forced to get a part time JOB or have to find a way to reduce your expenses.)

Of course, if you've made it this far in the book, you've probably guessed that I favor the choice of having people choose the other way by starting a part time business while working your full-time job and follow the blueprint of mastering your money. The great thing about doing it this way is, you won't necessarily have to be limited to the amount of passive income from your pension plan. As a matter of fact, when properly executed and with the right passive business, your passive income can continue to increase even during your retirement. This can help deal with the inflation problem that most people have. Best of all, as a final note on this method, in the event of your passing from this world as we know it, your passive income business can be passed on to the beneficiary of your estate. This passive income can be passed down to another generation. Your pension and social security will generally be passed on to your spouse or beneficiary and then that's it.

In closing, please note that this is only the beginning of your journey. There are more advanced techniques and advanced blueprints that you can follow, but my goal for this book was to simply get you started on your path to FINANCIAL FREEDOM. I believe that it is very important that you stop following the current financial path of most people and the same old teachings of society and make a change. (Assuming that you want more) I believe that building up a passive income stream in addition to your JOB is the way to go for many people. This can get you on the right track and you can make adjustments to the next level as you grow. I will be giving you some more information on the next level in another book and/or may have an area for you on the reference page. Either way, I want you to focus on getting yourself placed properly and ready to receive the next financial level of your journey.

At the end of the day or your desired retirement date, if you are an employee, you should have your retirement pension plan from your job (which is now passive) and the accumulated amount from your secondary pension plan which I suggested that you controlled, which by the way can/should be more than your jobs pension plan because you should've educated yourself over the years and accelerated that plan to at least double your jobs pension plan. With this lump sum, you can do as you please. You should also have built up an awesome passive stream of income from your part time business that will supplement your monthly payments from your retirement pension plan. Then, once you reach the age of collecting social security, that money will be like butter on a biscuit. All extra money for you to do even more things for others or yourself. Most of all, you should be debt free if you followed the blueprint over the years.

Always remember, YOU are your biggest asset! If you stay with the status quo and let someone else or the company control your financial future, you'll end up with one number/income for your retirement. On the other hand, if you educate yourself on how to master this game called money, you can retire with twice the amount or more by the time you reach retirement. Note: When I say educate yourself, I do not mean enrolling back in school to get another degree. I think that would be a waste of time and money. When I say educate yourself, I truly mean "YOURSELF". Learn to draw from within that which is already there. Learn specific financial and personal growth information that will help you be more efficient towards the financial goals that you have for yourself. Don't be distracted by the shiny object syndrome of other people and businesses trying to sabotage you or to get you to contribute solely to their retirement plan. Stay Focused!

If by any chance you are reading this book and you've already balanced yourself financially and are ahead of this game, congrats to you. Sometimes I meet people that have made a great deal of money in a particular profession (Sports/Music/Acting/Corporate) or maybe came into some money by way of inheritance or lottery winnings. If that is the case and you need some assistance in maximizing your ROI, feel free to reach out to me on my reference page or social media. Also note that I will be writing a follow-up to this book with a more advanced but simple formula for building wealth. I purposely did not start with the wealth building formula because I believe it's not for everyone. However, I do believe that everyone can accomplish this first part of becoming financially free. It comes down to making a decision to just do it and not justifying any excuses.

Remember, everyone is following a financial plan for success. If you did not create one or if you are not following a blueprint like this built for your success, then you are probably following the financial plan that someone has for you to make them financially successful. Pay attention to your money. Where has it been going over the past months or years. That is the tail of the tape. That will let you know if you are working for your financial freedom or someone else's.

**You always have a choice**

When it's all said and done, you can look at this blueprint as something that you can or can't do. You can make a decision to try this blueprint or continue with your current plan. The stats are very clear. Look them up one day. It is said that 7.8 people are currently dependent on some form of government assistance by the time they reach the age of 65. That means you'll be a part of the Welfare System, Social Security System or some other government program designed to help the needy. Yup, that's 78 out of 100 people. Most of us already know that 3-5% of the people are the super wealthy and they pretty much run the world having more than enough money to survive, so if you're not in the top 5% of the wealthy folks, then there is a good chance that you'll end up in the 78 percent. Without a plan to succeed for yourself, it would be impossible for you to reach that 5 percent or the 17 percent in between the wealthy and the government supported 78%.

Just think about the final results that you can have if you follow the steps that I've laid out in the 60/40 plan. You could keep your current job if you like and you can retire with your pension plan, social security, your additional self-managed pension, a business with passive income which can be paying you 1k, 2k, 3k or even 5k per month depending on your goals. Note that this passive business can also be passed down to your children or other family members upon you passing away. What a great kick start in life for a family member. Remember that 100+ acres of land that my family used to have. Just think if my great great grandmother knew some of this information that I know. What a kick start we could've had. You'll also have your self- managed pension plan which could be paying you a monthly amount equal to or more than your jobs pension plan. At a minimum, it can supplement your job's pension plan. All by following the blueprint laid out in this book. A plus, plus, plus for you. No need for you to get a part time or full-time job after retirement. Who really wants to do that? I mean really!!! What's the point of working 25/30 or 40 years?

You can always get more money, you can always get another job, but "TIME" my friend is something that you can't get back. Once it has passed, it's gone, and you can't get that Time back. **Time is precious** and you would've already put your time in. Spend these years doing something that you really love. Do something that you "want to do" instead of "have to do". Volunteer somewhere, do for someone else, spend more time with family and/or travel the beaches of the world. Let it be your choice! You always have a choice!!

Ok, that's it. I'd like to thank you for reading this book. I pray that it's been enlightening for you in some manner and that you put it to good use into your financial life. Use this information to not only help yourself, but to help others also. Now that you've purchased this book for yourself. Purchase another one and give it to a friend, family member or children as a gift. Help them get on the road to FINANCIAL FREEDOM early in life. Help them learn How they can be MASTERING THIS GAME CALLED MONEY.

Good luck in the pursuit of your goals and dreams and finding your purpose in life.

John Jester


ps.
For your reference, I've placed some resources on a webpage. You can get there by going to

www.thisgamecalledmoney.com

# HOW DOES YOUR FINANCIAL FREEDOM PLAN LOOK?

What is your Financial Goal?     _____per Month

How much passive income do you currently have coming in towards that Goal?                    _____ per Month

What are your total current Expenses?    _____ per Month

YOUR FINANCIAL FREEDOM BEGINS WHEN YOUR PASSIVE INCOME EXCEEDS YOUR MONTHLY EXPENSES AND YOUR ADDITIONAL WANTS.  IF YOU HAVE NOT STARTED BUILDING YOUR PASSIVE INCOME, NOW IS THE TIME TO GET STARTED!

EX  $8,000 monthly passive income, minus $7,000 of expenses and extras, equals a positive cash flow of $1,000 passive income coming into your life.  You are officially FINANCIALLY FREE!  Keep Growing, Keep Building, Keep Investing, Live Life, Dream Big!

This income can be from your Job Pension, 401K, or even better, from a fund or business that you start separately and grow.  You'll be able to have more control and possibly reach your FINANCIAL FREEDOM FASTER,

AT THE END OF THE DAY, THE CHOICE IS ALWAYS UP TO YOU.  YOU ALWAYS HAVE A CHOICE!

## Personal Notes

# Personal Notes

# Personal Notes

www.ingramcontent.com/pod-product-compliance
Lightning Source LLC
Chambersburg PA
CBHW060357050426
42449CB00009B/1779